Additional Praise for
The Seven S.E.C.R.E.T.S. of the Money Masters

"We have used these ideas at Top Gun to focus and define our leadership to better serve all those we come in contact with. I heartily endorse this book as a useful guide to improving and strengthening your vision, leadership, and money-management. 7 Secrets is a great guide filled with wisdom, practical ideas, insights, and activities designed to make you think and grow."

—Robert Dean, Jr., International Network Marketing Guru

"7 Secrets is not just another book on money management. It is a truly useful guide to what the reader can and should do. The authors recognize that there is just as much power in developing a "money-mindset" as there is in understanding the mechanics of economic theory. I recommend this book to my organization and suggest you do the same."

—Bob Steed, CEO, Trivani International

"Robert Shemin has done it again! He (and his co-author) have taken some very complex and often intimidating subjects and made them very easy for the average American to fully understand. But even more important than this understanding is that he provides a plan; some action steps that anyone can take today to achieve and secure a healthy financial future. I would strongly recommend this book to anyone who needs a bit more clarity in their overall financial and investing life."

—Scott M. Estill PC, Of Counsel, Estill & Long, LLC

The Seven S.E.C.R.E.T.S.
of the Money Masters

The Seven S.E.C.R.E.T.S. of the Money Masters

Robert Shemin
and
Peter Hirsch

WILEY

John Wiley & Sons, Inc.

Published by John Wiley & Sons, Inc., Hoboken, New Jersey.
Published simultaneously in Canada.

For general information on our other products and services or for technical
support, please contact our Customer Care Department within the United
States at (800) 762-2974, outside the United States at (317) 572-3993 or
fax (317) 572-4002.

Wiley also publishes its books in a variety of electronic formats. Some content
that appears in print may not be available in electronic books. For more
information about Wiley products, visit our web site at www.wiley.com.

Library of Congress Cataloging-in-Publication Data

Shemin, Robert, 1963-
    The seven S.E.C.R.E.T.S. of the money masters / Robert Shemin and Peter
Hirsch.
       p.   cm.
    Includes index.
    ISBN 978-0-470-61518-8 (cloth); 978-0-470-92674-1 (ebk);
    978-0-470-92675-8 (ebk); 978-0-470-92676-5
       1. Finance, Personal. 2. Investments. I. Hirsch, Peter, 1965- II. Title.
    III. Title: Seven secrets of the money masters.
    HG179.S46143   2010
    332.024—dc22

                                                                2010032751

Printed in the United States of America
10 9 8 7 6 5 4 3 2 1

For Ariel, Malia, and Alexander

Contents

Contents

Preface

So it's a down economy, right? How often do we hear that? Would it surprise you to hear that we disagree? Before you put this book down, let us explain. You see, a down economy implies that there will be an up economy. Sure, there are waves and cycles. But there is something more important. There is YOU. Rather than thinking in terms of down or up, think in terms of CHANGED. We are living in an economy that is forever changed. Think of it this way: you are living in a PERSONAL economy; a VALUE-BASED economy. No matter what is going on around you, there remains the question of what is going on IN you. While it's important to be a student and to learn economic trends, conditions, and forecasts, Over and above that, there will always be YOU. So work on becoming better, more educated, and more valuable. Work on your personal economy. The reality is that you may need a better strategy.

Suppose you were given the opportunity to play in the Masters, the world's most prestigious golf tournament, and you were given two choices. You could pick the golfer you admired most—anyone from today's game or one of the all-time greats who are now retired or deceased—and take one of two things from him. You could have access to all of his equipment, including top-of-the-line clubs, custom-made shoes, even his expert caddy, or you could have his swing. Which would you choose?

If you were smart, you'd take the swing. Clubs, balls, and the other tools of the trade are just products, and every year something new and better comes along. Frankly, a top-ranked professional golfer could probably toss aside his clubs, break a limb off a tree alongside the fairway, and still beat you and me to the cup. But his swing—that's something that can't be duplicated. It's his philosophy, his strategy. It's what sets him apart from everyone else. It's what makes him a master.

What is a master? Very simply, it's someone who has done something over and over and over again until he or she is the best at it.

In today's financial landscape, there is no shortage of people who claim to be masters at helping us make the most of our money. You have probably received mail from several of them, perhaps inviting you to a complimentary lunch or dinner to learn how to stretch your retirement fund or ensure that your children can get an Ivy League education. Maybe you've been invited to an all-day seminar that claims to reveal a foolproof plan for turning $999 into $499,999.

If you suffer from insomnia, you've almost certainly come across late-night infomercials featuring so-called money masters who have developed a unique formula for getting free money from the federal government, picking winning stocks, or any of a hundred other wealth-producing schemes that *you, too, can access for the low price of $39.99, or just $29.99—if you're one of the first 50 callers!*

Every city's phone book has page after page of display ads for individuals and firms who want to provide you with financial advice. Do a Google search for "how to invest money" and you'll get nearly 12 million hits.

Your local bookstore undoubtedly has a large selection of books and magazines designed to help you manage your money, and of course every large newspaper has a financial section. There are even several television networks dedicated entirely to money, investing, and finance.

Do all these people qualify as masters? Of course not. In fact, there is a good chance that your own stockbroker or financial adviser is far, far less than a master, and perhaps doesn't know much more than you do about selecting the right investments for your personal situation.

As we'll demonstrate, many financial advisers are better at selling their services than they are at actually helping you make sound decisions. They stride down the fairway with confidence because they're equipped with the newest, shiniest set of golf clubs, but they lack one important thing—the knowledgeable, skilled, practiced swing of a master.

Don't get the wrong idea; we're not in favor of loading all the stockbrokers and financial advisers onto a bus and driving it over a cliff. Some are honest, forthright, hard-working individuals who have an in-depth understanding of how money works and who are in a position to help their clients build financial security and even wealth. Some are masters.

But the simple fact is that many are not. In an age in which anyone can rent out a storefront office and claim to be a financial adviser, it's not always easy to separate the wheat from the chaff. Even worse, many of these "advisers" are less than honest with their clients about important information that can make a big difference in how a portfolio performs—information like the myriad of fees and expenses that are attached to many investment vehicles, and even how they, our financial advisers, earn their money.

The goal of this book is not to make you a money master overnight. That's impossible. Our goal is to share with you some of the information that true money masters know, understand, and use to their advantage, but that hasn't necessarily been passed along to the rest of us.

The Seven Secrets of the Money Masters is not a get-rich-quick scheme or a list of specific investments guaranteed to turn a few dollars into a fortune. What you'll learn in the following pages will help you become a more astute investor and a better steward of your own money. In this book:

- You will learn how to tell the difference between a financial adviser who is a master and one who is simply a salesperson.
- We will tell you the little-known truth about the 401(k) and how keeping yours might be costing you your retirement.
- We will shed light on the shell game that allows Wall Street to advertise a 25 percent annual return for an account that is actually losing money.
- You will learn that while Uncle Sam might appear to be a kindly, benevolent uncle, he doesn't necessarily have your best interests at heart.
- We will show you how much money your investments might be costing. That's right—costing, not earning.

We have organized this book into an easy-to-remember acronym: SECRETS, which stands for Safety, Expense, Cash Flow, Rate of Return, Economy, Tax Efficiency, and Sense. That last one is common sense, and who couldn't use a little more of that in trying to navigate today's complex financial climate?

In addition to the seven secrets, you will also find some bonus material. In Appendix A, we suggest seven questions you should ask your financial adviser, and we also provide a list of recommended reading and other resources intended to help you manage your money, your time, and your life, as well as think more deeply about how the world around us works. We have also created a companion web site—www.the 7secrets.net. There you'll find more information about some of the topics discussed in this book as well as worksheets you can use.

And if you're currently drowning in debt, in Chapter 3 we give you access to our exclusive software that can help you eliminate your debt, including your mortgage, in just a few years and without living like a pauper.

Now a word about how *The Seven Secrets of the Money Masters* is structured. Each chapter contains two parts. First, we'll discuss one of the secrets and how it might be affecting your financial life. Then we'll tell you a story.

To illustrate how the seven secrets—individually and cumulatively—can be applied to real-world situations, we have created a group of fictional characters whose experiences will serve as examples of how money works in our lives, and how we can improve our lifestyles by learning and applying the information in this book.

You'll meet Michael, his father Ben, his girlfriend Melissa, and other friends and family members who face financial challenges that will probably mirror those you or someone you know is facing. It is our hope that by following their stories, you'll learn to make the kinds of decisions that will enable you to move from the ranks of the confused and clueless into that rare group of people who understand how their money works and know how to make it work harder for them.

Some of what you'll read in the following pages will contradict things your financial advisers have been telling you for years. That's the point. In a time of economic upheaval, it is important to question the conventional wisdom that got us into our current situation, both as individuals and as a global community.

Other information will probably sound familiar to you. We talk about some money management practices and techniques that have been recommended for years, but before you brush them aside, ask yourself this: Are you really applying them? And if you were, would you have more financial security? Would you worry less about the future? Good ideas aren't worth much if you're not carrying them out in your daily life.

So are you ready? Let's get started!

Acknowledgments

We'd like to thank our families for their continuous love, encouragement, and support while we traveled the world sharpening these principles. Additionally, our literary agent, David Hale Smith, has been a source of constant wisdom, as have the staff and editors at John Wiley & Sons, whose feedback has been invaluable. Also, Josh Spivey of Lisert Financial in Dallas, who understands economic trends as well as anyone we have worked with and was a source of nonstop education for both of us. Last, Susan McDonald, who helped us turn these thoughts and stories into coherent words on the pages you're reading.

The Seven S.E.C.R.E.T.S. of the Money Masters

The Skinny Cow

Some 3,000 years ago, a poor farmer named Adir lived with his wife and three children in a small village about 50 miles from Jerusalem. He was a subsistence farmer, working hard to get the most out of his tiny plot of land, but he was barely managing to feed his family.

His neighbors were equally poor, and although they liked and admired Adir, they were envious of him because he had something they lacked—a cow. This cow was nothing like the robust cattle we might see when driving through the countryside today. On the contrary, she was skinny and looked a bit sickly, but the small amount of milk Adir was able to get from her a couple of times each week gave him something to trade for other items that kept his family going. Needless to say, he was very grateful for the cow and never considered slaughtering her, although the meat would have provided several meals for the family.

One day, a well-known spiritual leader entered Adir's village, along with a small group of followers and students.

1

The man was called Ba'al Shem Tov. In the Hebrew language Ba'al means master, Shem means name, and Tov means good.

Adir was a very spiritual man, so he was quite excited when word spread that the Ba'al Shem Tov was in his village, and absolutely thrilled when the great leader approached his shabby home and stopped in front. His excitement turned to shock when the Ba'al Shem Tov announced that he and his followers were tired from the day's travels and asked if they could spend the night at Adir's home.

Adir's first reaction was pride that this much-admired spiritual leader had chosen his humble farm, but his pride was immediately replaced by embarrassment when he realized how little he had to offer. Surely the Ba'al Shem Tov was accustomed to far greater accommodations, but his apologies were brushed aside and the Ba'al Shem Tov walked into the small house, followed by his students. Adir's wife watched in horrified silence, but it was clear that the Ba'al Shem Tov intended to stay.

Bad turned to worse when the Ba'al Shem Tov announced that he and his followers were hungry, and asked what the family had available for dinner. Remember that Adir could barely feed his own family, so providing a meal for nine grown men seemed out of the question. He consulted with his wife, suggesting that their only hope was to slaughter their skinny, but prized, cow. She protested, reminding her husband that once the cow was gone, so was the milk that had been enabling the family to survive, but in the end, they realized they had no other choice.

Adir reluctantly slaughtered and butchered the cow, thinking it would provide enough meat for their guests' dinner with some left over to feed his family for a few more days, but that plan quickly vanished when the meal was set out.

The Ba'al Shem Tov was a wonderful guest, entertaining the group with amazing stories, but Adir watched in growing dismay as the great man ate four or five times as much as anyone else. Within two hours, every morsel of meat had been consumed. There would be nothing left over.

The Ba'al Shem Tov had one surprise left. As soon as he'd finished eating, he stood up and announced that he'd changed his mind about spending the night. He felt sufficiently rested to walk a few more miles, so as quickly as they'd arrived, he and his followers vanished into the night.

Adir's head was spinning. Everything had happened so quickly and he hadn't had time to process any of it. Unable to cope with his growing despair, he left the house and headed into the adjacent forest to clear his head.

As he was walking through the woods, wondering how he would take care of his family now that the cow was gone, he heard a noise just ahead. Walking further, he came upon an older man who was lying on the ground and moaning in pain. When Adir approached, the man said he'd fallen and injured his leg, and now he was unable to walk. Never one to abandon someone in need, Adir walked to a nearby stream and returned with water for the stranger to drink. As they sat on the ground, wondering what to do next, the men began to talk, beginning with the customary exchange of names.

When Adir heard the stranger's name—Mordechai— he immediately recognized it. This was the wealthiest man in the province. Adir asked if the stories he'd heard about Mordechai were true—that he lived in an enormous palace, had dozens of servants, and owned countless businesses.

"Yes, that's all true," Mordechai replied.

"That's amazing," Adir said. "You're the most fortunate man in the world."

"Not really," Mordechai said. "It's true that I have a lot of money and possessions, but that's all my family cares about. To tell you the truth, they're just waiting for me to die so they

can get their hands on everything I have. In fact, they'd probably be pretty excited if they knew I was stranded here in the
woods, injured with no way to get home. Nothing would make
them happier than for me to die alone out here."

Adir thought about his own wife and children. They didn't
have much—and with the cow gone, they now had even less
than before—but they loved and took care of each other, and
helped their neighbors when they could. He couldn't imagine
living any other way.

Adir crafted a makeshift splint and tied it to Mordechai's
ankle by tearing his own shirt into strips, then helped the
injured man to the home of the nearest neighbor. Borrowing
a donkey and cart, Adir took Mordechai to a town some ten
miles away, where Mordechai had a business acquaintance
who promised to take him the rest of the way home.

"I can't thank you enough for your kindness" Mordechai
said as the two men parted ways. "All anyone cares about is
my money. You're the first person who has helped me without
expecting anything in return. I won't forget it."

Three years later, while on another pilgrimage, the Ba'al
Shem Tov passed through Adir's village again. By now, his followers had grown to more than 100, including the original
group who had visited Adir's home on their previous trip.

As they were walking along the narrow dirt road, a commo-
tion arose and the group moved aside to make way for a large,
elegant carriage pulled by four fine-looking horses. Intrigued
that such a vehicle would be in this impoverished area, the
students peered inside as the carriage passed by. They were
stunned to see Adir and his wife.

Recognizing the group, Adir stopped the carriage and got
out to speak to his old acquaintances. The students had plenty
of questions, and they were surprised to learn that the source of
Adir's newfound riches was Mordechai, who had died several

months earlier and left his fortune to the only person who had seen beyond his wealth and power.

The Ba'al Shem Tov had said little, and after Adir's carriage continued down the road, the students were curious about his knowing smile.

"We've wondered about this among ourselves," one said. "Your behavior that night was out of character. You rarely eat meat, yet you ate an enormous amount that night, even though you knew that family had very little food. And it's unlike you to go back on your word, but you got up and left as soon as dinner was over, even though you'd planned to spend the night. That family was so poor, and yet you treated them pretty shabbily."

"They weren't poor," the Ba'al Shem Tov said. "They were actually very wealthy. The only thing standing in their way was that skinny cow. I had to get rid of it."

◆ ◆ ◆

That sickly, skinny cow had been the sole focus of Adir's attention. He was terrified to let it go because he was convinced that he needed it, but once it was eliminated, he could see the bigger picture and move forward.

As you read through the following chapters, think carefully about what your skinny cows might be. We all have one or more, and in this book we'll try to help you recognize yours and get rid of them.

Skinny cows come in many forms. For some people, they are something tangible, such as a particular stock that we inherited from a beloved grandfather and refuse to sell even though it's unlikely to ever perform well again.

Maybe yours is your stockbroker. His kids go to school with your kids and you see him regularly at various events, so you're reluctant to cut him loose despite the fact that your investments are losing money and you've lost all faith in him.

Many people hang onto false ideas and money myths. They think that rich people got that way because they're simply smarter than the rest of us, or that it's necessary to have a lot of money in order to make a lot more money.

Fear can be a crippling skinny cow. Fear of making a mistake, fear of choosing the wrong investments, fear of asking questions, fear of looking foolish—all hold us back if we don't face them head-on and slaughter them.

We've known a great many people who are procrastinators. They put off saving for the future, getting their debts under control, talking to their spouses about their family's financial position, or taking a hard look at how their investments are performing and making adjustments if necessary.

Keep this story in mind as you continue reading. Try to recognize your skinny cow—or perhaps you're holding onto more than one. Whatever your skinny cow turns out to be, it's time to see that cow for what it really is and admit that it's holding you back.

CHAPTER 1

Michael's Very Bad Day

Michael Guilford was in a hurry. He was meeting his girlfriend, Melissa, at their favorite Thai restaurant for dinner, and he was already running late when he rushed to the automatic teller machine in the lobby of his bank. He quickly stuck his card into the slot, punched in his four-digit code, and selected the $40 quick cash option. He tapped his fingers impatiently on the machine as he waited for the money to appear, but instead of the familiar sound of $20 bills being shuffled electronically, he heard a short series of clicks before the machine spit out his card and a slip of paper.

Insufficient funds.

"You've got to be kidding," Michael muttered to himself. "That can't possibly be right. My paycheck was just deposited a few days ago."

Putting his card forcefully back into the ATM, he repeated the process, this time asking for just $20. The result was the same.

Now what? With a sick feeling in the pit of his stomach, he pulled out his cell phone and called the first number on his speed dial. Melissa answered after two rings and Michael sputtered out a clumsy story about having to work late . . . couldn't make it for dinner . . . so sorry . . . he'd make it up to her tomorrow. He felt like scum lying to her, but there was no way he could face her right now. She would probably be understanding, like she always was, but that would just make him feel worse.

Michael walked to the parking garage adjacent to his office building, took the elevator to the fourth level, and headed to his assigned space. As he walked, he checked his wallet. Four dollars. Thank God he had a monthly parking pass. With the high price of parking in downtown Chicago, the attendant would have laughed at his meager four dollars.

As he drove home, Michael kept a nervous eye on the gas gauge, which showed that the tank was dangerously close to being empty. He let out an audible sigh of relief when he pulled into the garage at his condominium. Thanks to the unusually light traffic, he'd made it, but he'd need gas in the morning. Either that or walk seven blocks to the nearest El station, and the way his luck was running, there would be a driving rainstorm.

Tossing the day's mail onto the kitchen table, Michael noticed that the top envelope bore his bank's return address. He opened it to find a form letter admonishing him that his account was overdrawn by $125.57. The letter politely instructed him to deposit funds immediately to cover the amount, and mentioned that he'd been charged a $50 overdraft fee and $5 per day until the account was in the black again.

"Pleasure doing business with you," he said bitterly as he wadded up the letter and angrily stuffed it into the trash can.

His answering machine was blinking with more bad news. His MasterCard bill was late again and a recorded message sternly asked him to call an 800 number to discuss the matter. He hit the delete button without writing down the number.

Michael went into the second bedroom that served as his home office and booted up his computer. Might as well face it, he thought as he logged onto his bank's web site and accessed his account.

There it was. The record of his recent transactions clearly showed that he was, in fact, broke. Glancing through the list, the sick feeling returned as he watched his most recent paycheck gradually disappear in a matter of four days. His eyes raked down the screen as he forced himself to study his transactions for the past month. There was the automatic draw for the mortgage on the condo, a number of cash withdrawals, and a lengthy list of point-of-purchase transactions. Restaurants, clothing stores, the coffee shop in his office building, the list went on and on. No question about it, no one had siphoned money from his account or stolen his identity. He'd made this mess all by himself.

Instead of enjoying a spicy chicken curry and a bottle of wine with Melissa, Michael made a peanut butter sandwich and returned to his desk. Maybe it was time to figure out just how much financial trouble he was in. He reached for his calculator, then opened the bottom drawer of the desk and pulled out the stack of bills and bank statements he'd been dropping in there. Many of the envelopes hadn't even been opened.

After an hour of sorting out his bills and adding up the numbers, Michael felt more dismayed than ever. Two of his credit cards were maxed out and the third was close. He was two months behind on all of them and the minimum payment amounts had become staggering. No wonder he'd been throwing the bills into the drawer unopened. Looking at them was too upsetting, so it was easier to avoid it altogether. The cable bill was perpetually a month behind, and he always paid the past due balance just a day or so before his service was scheduled to be suspended. There were other bills—a department store charge card, his student loan, his cell phone—all with looming due dates even though his bank account was empty.

Meanwhile, there was the immediate problem of finding enough cash to get through the rest of the week. Michael stood up and walked to the window. He dug his hands into his pockets dejectedly, and began idly fingering the coins he found there.

"Change!" he said out loud.

Hurrying into his bedroom, Michael headed for the closet and pulled down a large jar into which he dropped his loose change every night. It was about two-thirds full.

He felt like a complete idiot, skulking out of the building like some kind of thief, with a jar of coins under his arm. He drove to the nearest grocery, dumped the change into the big green machine near the entrance, and listened as the coins were sorted and counted. Finally a slip of paper emerged. Michael let out a sigh of relief. $88.50. That would be enough. He walked quickly to the customer service desk to get his cash.

While driving home, Michael's thoughts returned to his overall situation. How had things gotten this bad? He was an accountant, for heaven's sake. He understood numbers and he was good at them. Just five years out of college, he earned a fairly healthy paycheck, but he never seemed to be able to get ahead. Buying the condo might have been a mistake because the mortgage payment was pretty steep, but he'd told himself that it was smart to own rather than rent. It was an investment in his future. He was plowing the maximum into his 401(k) and always had his eyes open for other investment opportunities, although he didn't have a clue where he'd get the cash in the event that a good one came along. He and Melissa had talked about marriage, but had no firm plans yet, and neither of them was in a rush. It was probably just as well. He had the impression that her parents weren't in a position to finance a big wedding, and Michael obviously couldn't do it at this point.

When he got home, Michael returned the now-empty jar to the closet shelf and went back into the office. He shoved the stack of bills into a manila folder, along with the legal pad containing the numbers he'd been totaling, and leaned back in his chair to consider his options. His next paycheck would be deposited on Friday, but it wouldn't begin to cover all these bills, and the overdraft fees would come off the top. Getting a bank loan seemed unlikely, given what he assumed was the current state of his credit rating. There was no way he could ask Melissa to bail him out. He didn't even know how much she made because they never discussed money.

He could think of only one option. Michael took a deep breath, picked up the phone, and dialed his parents' number.

"Hey, Dad. I've got . . . an issue. Can I come by and talk to you tomorrow?"

◆ ◆ ◆

The following morning, Michael called his office to say he would be late, then tossed a sandwich and an apple into his briefcase. No restaurant lunches for him for a while. After putting $20 worth of fuel into his car's tank, he drove downtown to his father's office.

Ben Guilford was a successful attorney with an office overlooking busy Michigan Avenue. He wasn't wealthy, but he'd been careful with his money and looked forward to a comfortable retirement in a few years. He and his wife were eying a condominium community in a suburb of Phoenix, where they could escape the brutal Chicago winters and play golf year-round.

Nervously entering his father's office, Michael felt like he was 16 years old again and about to confess to denting the fender of his dad's car. It was one thing to call home from college to ask for more money. Now he was too old for this.

Ben listened quietly as Michael explained his situation. As he began to wind up his spiel, Michael pulled the legal pad from his briefcase and pushed it across the desk.

"So that's the total," he said, feeling his cheeks burning. It was so humiliating. "If you could help me even a little bit, I'd really appreciate it. And of course I'll pay you back. I'm not sure when, but I will."

Ben looked at the numbers on the pad, raising his eyebrows almost imperceptibly, and reached for his checkbook. Michael felt his body begin to relax for the first time since he left the ATM the day before.

"That's not enough to pay off all your debts, as you can see, but it will get all your bills current and carry you for another month or so," Ben said as he handed the check to his son.

"Oh, that's fine, Dad. Anything to get me liquid again will be great. I can't thank you enough, and now I'll let you get back to work," Michael said as he stood up to leave. His father had been more than gracious, but Michael couldn't wait to put an end to this embarrassing conversation and get the check into the bank.

"Not so fast," Ben said, signaling his son to sit back down. "I want to tell you a story about a dog."

Michael mentally rolled his eyes. He should have known there would be a high price for this.

Ben leaned back in his chair and began. "When I was growing up in Texas, there was a guy in our little town named Mr. Scott, who drove around with his dog riding in the bed of his pickup truck. The truck was pretty shabby, and there was always a lot of junk in the back. One summer when I was in high school, I worked at a gas station, and this guy would stop by once a week or so, and the dog would always be in the back of the truck, howling and yelping like crazy.

"One afternoon, Mr. Scott came by for gas, and the dog was in the back of the truck as usual, but this time he was perfectly calm and quiet. I couldn't resist asking what had happened. 'The pain got too bad,' he said. He went on to explain that there had been a board in the back of the truck, and it had several nails sticking out of it. The dog had gotten into the habit of sitting on the board, even though the nails were digging into his rump, but although it hurt, he'd never bothered moving because the pain wasn't bad enough. When it finally became unbearable, he moved.

"You're a little bit like that dog, Michael. Your precarious financial situation keeps you in a lot of pain, but most of the time it's not enough to get you to move off the nails. That check will get you back on your feet, but it's time for you to recognize the full extent of the pain you're in and do something about it. Clearly you have a lot of capabilities, but you've got to stop being so irresponsible. Of course I'm happy to help you, but this issue goes beyond your immediate cash flow problem."

Michael opened his mouth to speak, but his father held up his palm. "I'm not finished. My concern is that you're going to end up right back in this same situation if you don't start getting smart about money, so I'm going to help you do that. Don't make any plans for the next couple of Sunday afternoons. You're going to be spending them with me. Bring all your financial records. We're going to start getting you on the right track."

The 7 S.E.C.R.E.T.S

Safety

Suppose we were to ask you, "What is the first thing you need to do in order to attain financial security and build wealth?" What would your response be? If you're like most people, you'd probably say, "Earn more money and invest wisely."

And you'd be wrong.

The first step in getting control of your financial life is ensuring that what you already have, regardless of how much or how little that may be, is protected. Many people are so focused on getting more that they forget to take the necessary steps to preserve their current assets until it's too late.

Protecting your money is even more important than making more of it, because once you get behind, it's very difficult to catch up. Let's look at a simplified example.

Suppose you buy 100 shares of Widgets, Inc. stock at $1 a share. During the first six months of your investment, Widgets' top competitor introduces a hot new product and the value of Widgets' stock drops by 50 percent. But there's good news on the horizon. A few months down the road, Widgets comes out with an even hotter product and the stock doubles in value. Great, right? Not so fast. After the first hit, your stock was worth only $50, so your 100 percent profit only gets you back to your original $100. You're barely breaking even. That's why it's important to avoid loss if at all possible, because once you're in a hole, it's very difficult to climb back out.

Unfortunately, a no-risk investment simply doesn't exist, but there are ways to determine the level of risk before getting involved.

Investigate before You Invest

Don't make a move without taking the time and energy necessary to investigate the stability of the business itself, the person or people behind it, and the banks or other investors providing back-up at the next level. Remember that size isn't always an indicator of stability. You have to look no further than the Big Three U.S. auto companies to see that even very large, seemingly stable businesses aren't immune to devastating losses.

When we're making a business decision, we live by a simple principle and suggest that you do the same: Investigate, verify, and verify again.

We strongly recommend looking into the background of anyone with whom you're considering doing business. That might sound cynical, but we've seen far too many people lose enormous amounts of money by trusting the wrong person or business entity.

Just as leopards and other animals display patterns as part of their physical appearance, people develop patterns of behavior that we should be aware of in order to keep our businesses, investments, and relationships safe. Just as a leopard doesn't change his spots, someone with a history of nefarious business dealings or questionable financial practices is unlikely to change, so make sure you know who you're getting into bed with when your money is at stake.

Not so many years ago, it was relatively easy for people to hide a great deal about themselves, but that isn't the case today. Thanks to modern technology, it's no longer necessary to hire a private investigator to get basic information on someone. There are simple Internet tools that, for a very small fee, will allow you to verify almost any piece of information, from someone's driving record to credit history and criminal record. Before you hire a new employee, rent property to a new tenant, or go into an investment with a partner, it just makes sense to find out who you're dealing with. The information is out there, but you have to take personal responsibility for finding it.

How Volatile Is the Investment?

The stock market is a great example of extreme volatility, and yet 98 percent of financial planners have no qualms about putting their clients' money, including their retirement accounts, into mutual funds despite the enormous risk involved. It should be illegal to have people nearing retirement exposed to full market risk. That is nothing short of financial malpractice.

We've all known people who have been sucked into investing large sums of money in the stock market based on tales of the huge profits being made by other investors. Around 1999, legends about dotcom millionaires and people who quit their jobs to find wealth as day traders, buying and selling Internet and technology stocks from their home computers, fostered the notion that the market was a modern-day gold rush.

These investors were riding high on confidence, convinced that they'd become money masters blessed with knowledge that would enable them to continue making huge sums of money indefinitely. We all know what happened next. As surely as night follows day, the dotcom bust followed the dot-com boom, and a lot of people lost a lot of money.

Then and now, it's easy to find people who will tell you they can predict the market. Brokerage houses spend tens of millions of dollars on advertising, ensuring you that they have specialized knowledge that will protect your investments and make them grow. Investment advisors will tell you they have found the key to timing the market and predicting which stocks will do well, and the financial programs on television love to trot out the latest wunderkind who has beaten the market and can tell you how it's done.

Make a note of that guy's name and keep watching. The chances are excellent that a year from now, he'll have faded away and been replaced by someone else. Some people do manage to beat the market, but hardly anyone is able to do it consistently. It's simply not possible to predict with regularity which stocks will go up and down, and when they will do it.

It's much like betting on the Kentucky Derby. You can study all the available information about how each horse has done in previous outings on a similar track in comparable weather conditions, but past performance is just that—past. It can provide clues, but it is not an indicator of how a particular horse will run today. There are no more reliable systems for predicting the stock market than there are for predicting the outcome of a horse race.

How Expert Is Your Financial Expert?

The "investigate and verify" principle also applies to choosing a financial advisor. Our friend Jason enjoys fine dining and, because he travels a great deal for both work and pleasure, he has an opportunity to experience some of the best restaurants across the United States and around the world.

Before he leaves on a trip, he carefully combs the Internet and a stack of magazines, looking for new restaurants in the place he'll be visiting, or perhaps an old favorite he hasn't patronized for a while. Once he arrives, he studies the menu and the wine list meticulously and asks the wait staff several questions before deciding what to order. Good food is important to him, so he takes time to do his homework in order to get exactly what he wants.

When it comes to choosing a financial advisor, on the other hand, Jason is remarkably careless. He selected his first firm on the basis of an expensive brochure he received in the mail. Several months later, when he was dissatisfied and disillusioned, he switched to a guy recommended by a colleague at his office, although he had no idea whether the advisor was suited to his own individual needs or how well he was performing for his co-worker.

Now he finds himself with a portfolio that doesn't match his expectations and a broker who won't return his calls because he's no longer making money from Jason's investments. If he put a fraction of the time he spends on planning his dining experiences into researching his investment strategies and the people who are helping plan them, his budget for dining out would grow considerably.

If a trusted friend or family member recommends a broker or investment advisor, there's nothing at all wrong with considering the advice, but ask questions before you part with a single dime. Find out how much your friend really knows about this person's qualifications and track record. Is the broker just a golfing buddy or a fellow PTA member, or does your friend have concrete knowledge about his or her professional credentials? Is it possible that the person making the recommendation is inflating the success rate of his own investments in an effort to appear more prosperous?

Whether you're acting on a recommendation or your own research, when you sit down to meet with a potential advisor, treat that first meeting like a job interview, but be certain you're the interviewer, not the applicant. Don't be afraid to ask questions. You're considering entrusting this person with managing your money. You have every right to know what training the adviser has received, what type of financial licenses he or she holds, how long the person has been a stockbroker or an independent adviser, whether any written complaints have been filed against him or his firm, and whether you'll be dealing directly with him or be passed off to a subordinate. Many people are not aware that in today's world, virtually anyone can rent an office, get some business cards printed, and call themselves a financial advisor. Make sure you're dealing with someone with the proper training, licensing, and experience, and there are only two ways to do that—ask questions, and then verify everything you're told. Someone who bristles at your questions, appears uncomfortable or as if his feelings are hurt, or simply tries to placate you with vague reassurances is not the right financial advisor for you, no matter how well your brother-in-law claims he's doing for him.

Another red flag to watch for during your interview is an advisor who tries to snow you with jargon. Financial dealings are intimidating to many people. The industry has a language all its own, and it's easy for someone with a bit of training to toss out terms like hedge ratio and earned surplus in an effort to appear knowledgeable, assuming that you won't ask questions.

Just as unscrupulous automobile mechanics test your knowledge of cars before giving you an estimate for repairs, some investment counselors subtly size up your knowledge of finance and investments, and they begin to salivate if they smell blood in the water. Certainly your advisor should know more than you do. Otherwise, why would you need him? But look for someone who takes time to explain the details, and be certain you're comfortable rather than accepting a "just trust me" attitude from the advisor.

Keep in mind that, first and foremost, most brokers and financial advisors are salespeople. Often they are hired by a large firm primarily because of their charm, confidence, and people skills. The job of such advisors—the way they make money for themselves and their firms—is by selling you investments on which they earn a commission or fee.

Are they all unscrupulous snake oil salesmen? Of course not, but they are in the business of sales, and part of their job is to sell you on the idea that you need their help in order to make the most of your money. It's important to become an educated consumer with the ability to decide for yourself who to trust and how much you need to be involved in your own financial decisions.

Remember that at the end of the day, after you've done your research and questioned a potential financial advisor about his or her credentials and experience, it's always best to trust your instincts. Most of us have a little voice that tells us if we're uncomfortable with someone, even if we can't quite put our finger on why. There is no shortage of people who want to help you manage your money. If everything looks good on paper, but something simply doesn't feel right, find someone else. You will sleep better at night knowing you are working with someone in whom you have confidence.

We talk more about this later when we give you seven questions (and a bonus) you need to ask your financial advisor.

Are All Your Eggs in One Basket?

Remember the spectacular collapse of Enron? In its wake, Congressional committees investigating the scandal heard heartbreaking testimony from a number of Enron employees, who had lost not only their jobs but also their life savings and any hope of a comfortable retirement. A retiree from Texas reported losing nearly $1.3 million. A 59-year-old lab technician who had devoted 25 years to Enron and its subsidiaries was just months from his planned retirement when the company collapsed, and he saw his 401(k) drop from more than $600,000 to just $11,000. A secretary watched with amazement as her 401(k) skyrocketed to nearly $3 million, only to evaporate when the company filed for bankruptcy in December 2001. In all, some 12,000 Enron employees lost $1.3 billion, in addition to their jobs.

Why did this happen? Sadly, in many cases, it happened because employees believed so strongly in their company and the executives who ran it that they invested virtually all of their retirement savings in Enron stock. It seemed like a good idea at the time because the company matched their contributions, but as we now know, accounting fraud brought down the organization, its employees, and their life savings. Lesson learned, but too late.

To be sure, loyalty to an employer is a thing to be valued, but it's a very poor investment strategy. It's an equally bad idea to plow everything into any one type of investment, whether it's the stock market, real estate, or stuffing it into your mattress. There is no such thing as a sure thing, and there is no company or industry that is immune to financial ups and downs. Diversifying your investments is absolutely key to protecting your assets.

There are other strategies for scattering your eggs among several baskets. You might consider holding some assets in your own name, some in the names of businesses and corporations you've established, and some in trusts that you've created. In case of a major lawsuit or even a messy divorce, having more than one asset base can protect you from being completely wiped out.

Is Keeping Your 401(k) Costing You Your Retirement?

The Employee Retirement Income Security Act (ERISA) of 1974 was signed by President Gerald Ford on September 2, 1974, Labor Day, and this legislation made 401(k)s possible. The Act was passed to help protect employees' retirement money from abuse by owners of businesses.

While the ERISA was passed under the guise of being a benefit to employees, it turned out that the majority of the benefits were in favor of the employer. There is a good reason that 401(k) plans are so popular with employers. They transfer the risk to the employee, as opposed to employer-funded pension plans that provided a guaranteed retirement benefit for each participant. The resulting impact started by the ERISA is not only leaving millions of people without a retirement plan, it is also forcing people to trust their financial future to the stock market.

Another problem is the limitation of offerings that most companies provide their employees for their 401(k) or retirement plans. The control and direction is really in the hands of whoever decides what the company offers.

Direct investing in gold, commodities, real estate, art, and other vehicles typically is not available through a 401(k) plan, yet these are viable options that can be an important part of an investment portfolio. In order to make use of those vehicles, one would need a self-directed IRA or pension plan.

Furthermore, most companies do not take enough time to educate their employees about investing and the true nature of 401(k) investing. As a result, many employees simply choose a mutual fund or two in a method that's not far removed from blind man's bluff or pin the tail on the donkey. Then they go about their business and trust that the matter of saving for retirement has been handled.

We discuss the impact of the 401(k)—and why it might not be the retirement panacea you've been led to believe—when we talk about the sixth secret, tax efficiency, in Chapter 7.

If you have any lingering doubts about the importance of safety, consider not just yourself, but the other people to whom you're responsible. Almost all of us have others who depend on us—spouses, children, aging parents, employees, investors, other stakeholders. The only thing worse than losing your own money is losing someone else's, so it's imperative to remember our responsibilities to others and take the necessary steps to keep our assets safe.

● ● ●

Michael and Melissa sat at the kitchen table in her apartment, eating fast food take-out and talking about the just-completed work day. Michael was winding up a lengthy tale about how grossly incompetent his firm's new junior associate was when he noticed that Melissa seemed a little anxious.

"So anyway, that was my day. What about you? You look like you're dying to say something," Michael said.

"I guess I am," Melissa said. "I got a letter today from the attorney who's handling my grandmother's estate." A month earlier, Michael had met some of Melissa's extended family for the first time when he accompanied her to Indianapolis for her grandmother's funeral. While not unexpected, the death had been a blow to Melissa because the two had been close.

"Oh yeah? Did she leave you something?"

"She left me $20,000. Can you believe that?"

"Seriously? I didn't realize she had that kind of money."

"I didn't either, really. I mean, my grandfather worked in a factory, so he certainly never got wealthy, but I guess they were part of that generation that lived through the Depression and it affected them for the rest of their lives. I've told you how frugal Gram was. She clipped coupons and meticulously went through the grocery ads every week. After my grandfather retired, he'd drive her to three or four different groceries so she could get the lowest price on bananas here and paper towels there. We tried to tell her that they probably spent more on gas than they were saving, but she liked doing it. She even saved wrapping paper from birthday parties, ironed it and used it again."

"Sounds like my mom's mother," Michael said with a laugh. "She washed aluminum foil and reused it, and she measured her dishwashing liquid into a teaspoon because she didn't want to use too much."

"They would have been good friends! Anyway, I guess she and my grandfather saved a lot of money over the years because she had more than $150,000 in certificates of deposit alone when she died. She left $20,000 to each of her grandchildren and the rest to my parents and a couple of charities."

"What are you going to do with it?" Michael asked.

"I have no idea. It was completely unexpected. I never thought I'd have a lump sum of money like that."

"Well, it's a good problem to have," Michael replied, trying not to sound bitter or sarcastic. He still hadn't worked up the courage to tell her about his recent brush with destitution, and he wasn't sure he ever would, especially now. Although he and Melissa didn't talk about money, he had the impression that she managed hers well, even though he was pretty sure she made less than he did. The relationship was going well, so why rock the boat by letting her know what an idiot he was?

Melissa's voice interrupted his train of thought. "You're an accountant. Maybe you can tell me what I should do."

Michael laughed. "Just because I'm good with figures doesn't mean I know anything about taking care of money. Two different things. Two entirely different things. Hey, did you get a new movie from Netflix yet?" It was time to change the subject.

◆ ◆ ◆

The next day, the people from Melissa's department went out for lunch to celebrate a co-worker's birthday. Growing tired of hearing the latest details of Rita's divorce drama, Melissa turned toward the conversation on her left side.

"I'm telling you, this guy is a miracle worker," Rick was saying. "He's got me invested in a whole new group of stocks that I'd never considered before. We're buying and selling all the time. I'm telling you, I'm going to be able to retire early at this rate. You can all come and visit me at my house in Hawaii."

"Yeah, good luck with that," Dave said with a laugh.

Later in the afternoon, Melissa stopped by Rick's office and tapped lightly on the door frame.

"Got a minute?"

"Sure, what's up?"

"I heard you talking about your broker at lunch. You really like him?"

"He's fantastic. I don't know anything about this kind of stuff at all, so I just leave it up to him and he takes care of me. So far, I'm doing great. He knows all about timing the market, when certain stocks are going to go up and down, the whole thing. I don't know what he's talking about half the time, but I'm making money, so who cares? Are you looking for a broker?"

"Maybe. I just came into a bit of an inheritance and I haven't figured out what to do with the money yet. I don't know the first thing about investing, so I'm not sure where to even start."

Rick opened the middle drawer of his desk and pulled out a business card.

"Here you go. Give this guy a call. Tell him I sent you. He'll fix you right up."

"Okay, I'll call and make an appointment. Thanks."

"No problem. Maybe you can get a house next to mine on the beach when we both retire in style."

"Sounds like a plan," Melissa said as she turned and walked back to her office.

◆ ◆ ◆

Two days later, Melissa entered the plush offices of Morrow and Daniels Wealth Management LLC. The company occupied two floors of a high-rise office building in the heart of Chicago's financial district, and everything about the large reception area spelled success. The furniture was mahogany, the chairs and couches were upholstered in deep shades of burgundy and hunter green, and there were large arrangements of fresh flowers on several of the tables. An attractive receptionist greeted her warmly, and after a five-minute wait she was ushered into the office of Perry Blackman.

While not as opulent as the reception area, Blackman's office was nothing to complain about. It featured a large window facing Wabash Avenue, and there was a small round conference table in addition to two armchairs facing his desk. Melissa thought about her tiny, windowless hole back at the ad agency where she worked as a graphic designer. Someday, when she became creative director, she'd have an office like this.

Blackman was on the phone, but smiled broadly and motioned for her to sit down. "I can't urge you enough to jump on this opportunity," he was saying. "This one's a guaranteed winner."

Melissa took advantage of the opportunity to look around the office. There were photos of Blackman's family—a professional portrait showing him with his wife and two children, the children's most recent school pictures, a shot of his son holding a baseball trophy, and one of his daughters diving into the pool behind what was apparently his large suburban home. On the wall behind the conference table was a collection of plaques, one of which proclaimed Blackman's membership in something called the Ambassadors Club, including small brass plates indicating that he'd been in the organization each of the past six years.

"Okay then, I'll get the order in this afternoon. You won't be sorry. Say hi to Jenny for me, and I guess we'll see you Saturday. Take care."

Blackman returned the phone to its cradle, stood up and held out his hand. He took Melissa's hand in both of his and squeezed it firmly.

"I'm sorry about that. I'm Perry Blackman. Nice to meet you, Melissa."

"No problem at all. Impressive!" she said, gesturing toward the wall of plaques.

"Oh, I've been lucky. Those things don't mean much. I just like helping people like you make money. So Rick gave you my name. Great guy, isn't he?"

Melissa had been a little nervous about the meeting, especially since she knew nothing about how stockbrokers worked, but this guy was so friendly and engaging. She relaxed into her chair and they chatted for a few minutes about Rick and his penchant for practical jokes.

When the conversation turned back to the reason for her visit, Melissa explained that she'd recently inherited some money and was trying to decide what to do with it.

"How much?" Blackman asked.

"$20,000," Melissa replied, watching him jot the figure down on the pad in front of him.

"And have you invested in the market before?"

"No, I really don't know much about it, but Rick said you're the expert, so I thought I'd see what you recommended."

For the next ten minutes, Melissa listened as Blackman talked about index funds, convertible bonds, IPOs, the S&P, and a number of other terms that she didn't understand. He might as well have been speaking Mandarin Chinese.

"Do you have any questions?" Blackman asked.

Melissa laughed nervously. "I guess I'm not sure what to ask. This is all really foreign to me."

"I understand completely," Blackman said with a warm smile. "Let me boil it down. I think the best thing would be to put you in a growth fund that we've had a lot of success with." He leafed through a pile of papers on his desk, pulled out a brochure, and handed it to Melissa.

Melissa looked hesitantly at the brochure. It was a glossy piece and she knew from her work at the agency that no cost had been spared in producing it. Blackman was talking about the fund, again in terms that left her bewildered, as did the table of figures at the back of the brochure.

"The sooner you get invested in this, the sooner you'll start making money, so if you'll just get me a cashier's check for the $20,000, we'll get you started," Blackman said.

This was moving really fast. Blackman seemed knowledgeable, and he was certainly sure of himself, but she hadn't planned on turning the money over to him today. Still, he clearly knew more than she did, so why not just leap?

Before she could respond, Melissa's cell phone rang. She pulled it out of her bag and looked at the number.

"I'm sorry. It's my office. I'll just be a minute," she said.

"Don't worry about it. Take your time."

After a brief conversation, Melissa ended the call and turned back to Blackman. "I'm sorry, but I need to go. One of our big clients had signed off on a new logo I created and now they want to make changes and . . . it's a long story, but I need to get back to the office."

"Oh, I understand completely. Our clients have to come first, don't they? You just get me that check in the next day or two, and we'll start making you rich, okay?"

He walked her to the elevator and gave her another warm handshake.

"Charming guy," Melissa thought as the elevator doors closed.

◆ ◆ ◆

That evening, Melissa met Michael and his parents for dinner at a downtown restaurant.

"This is the first time we've seen you since your grand-mother's death, Melissa," Ben said. "Are you doing all right?"

"Yes. I miss her, but she'd been sick for quite a while. This always sounds so trite when people say it, but in a way it really was a blessing."

"Have you decided what to do with the money she left you?" Michael asked. He regretted the words the minute they left his mouth. Her inheritance wasn't his parents' business and she might not want them to know, and talking about money in front of his father might not be the smartest thing to do under the circumstances. Surely his dad wouldn't mention Michael's situation.

Melissa didn't seem to mind the question.

"Actually, I met with a stockbroker today," she said. "He seemed very knowledgeable and he's going to invest the money in some mutual fund he's high on. He explained it all to me, but most of it went over my head, so I guess I'll just let him handle it."

"Who's the broker?" Ben asked. "Maybe I know him."

"His name is Perry Blackman and he's with a firm called Morrow and Daniels. Their offices are on Wabash."

"I know the firm, but not the broker," Ben said. "How did you find him?"

"A guy at work recommended him. I liked him. He's really personable and his office is full of all kinds of plaques and awards, so I guess he must be good."

Ben paused for a moment, briefly debating with himself about the wisdom of pursuing the conversation. He liked Melissa enormously, but money was a dangerous topic and he didn't want to offend her.

"Good," Ben said. "So the two of you worked out a plan that meets your goals?"

"Goals?"

"You know, what you expect from your investments. Whether you're looking for long-term growth or short-term profits, how much risk you're willing to take on, that kind of thing."

Melissa hesitated.

"No, we didn't' talk about any of that. He pretty much just explained to me how he works, and then he gave me some information about the mutual fund he wants to put my money into." Suddenly she was feeling less confident about Mr. Blackman.

"Really? That's surprising because . . . well, never mind," Ben said.

"Mr. Guilford, I know nothing about this kind of thing. I've never had money to invest. I've never spoken to a stockbroker before. I don't know anything about the market or how it works, and I've never thought about the kind of investment goals you're talking about. If you have questions or concerns, please tell me. I've got a lot of respect for you, so I'd appreciate any help you've got to offer. It won't offend me, I promise. My grandmother left this money to me and I don't want to squander it just because I'm an idiot."

"You're hardly an idiot," Ben laughed. "We've just got different knowledge bases. I couldn't design my way out of a paper bag."

"Please," Melissa said, "tell me what you think."

Michael and his mother exchanged an amused look. Ben was about to launch into one of his favorite topics. There would be no stopping him now.

"The thing you have to understand about stockbrokers is that they are sales people first and foremost. This guy . . . what was his name? Blackman?"

"Yes."

"Mr. Blackman's job isn't really to help you make money. I'm sure he'd be happy for you if your investment with him paid off, but in the long run, he's a salesman. He has one job and one job only, and that's to sell investments to you and his other customers."

"But won't he make more money if I make more money?"

"No, because that's not how he gets paid. He's paid on commission. He and his firm get a fee when you buy or sell a security, so from a financial perspective it really doesn't make much difference whether your investment performs well for you. He's already earned his fee and moved on."

Melissa thought about the photos she'd seen on Blackman's credenza. He must be earning a lot of fees from a lot of customers to be able to afford a house like that.

"But he had all kinds of plaques hanging on the wall in his office," Melissa said. "I assumed they had something to do with him being the best at helping his clients make money, right?"

"Not really," Ben replied. "I'm pretty sure they mean he's earned more money for his company than his colleagues have. Those kinds of awards usually don't have anything to do with how his customers' investments are performing. They speak more to his success at improving the firm's bottom line, not yours."

"Oh. That's kind of disturbing."

"I'm not saying that this Blackman guy isn't honest or that he isn't good at helping his customers choose the right investments," Ben said quickly. "I have no idea whether he's any good or not. I'm just saying that a lot of brokers have more charm and personality than financial acumen. Did he mention to you what his credentials are?"

"No, I don't think so." Melissa's forehead crinkled a little as she tried to remember what she'd seen in Blackman's office. "He had his college diploma framed on his wall. I don't remember what his degree was in, but I don't think it was anything business related. I'd just noticed that when he got off the phone and we started talking, so I forgot about it completely, even though it surprised me at the time. I just assumed all brokers had a degree in business or finance."

"That's not unusual," Ben said. "I once knew a stockbroker who was a physical education major. He went through college on a basketball scholarship and barely graduated at all, but he sure knew how to charm people."

"Yeah, Mr. Blackman certainly has that going for him," Melissa replied. "He exudes an air of confidence, so I took it for granted that he was an expert in all of this stuff."

"And he might be," said Ben. "I guess the part that bothers me the most is that he didn't take time to talk with you about what your goals were. I'm a little dubious about how he knew what mutual fund to recommend without knowing more about what you were looking for from your investment."

"I didn't think about that, but you're right."

"Did he ask you any questions at all?"

"He asked me how much money I had to invest. That was it."

"Did you give him the money yet?"

"No, not yet. Our meeting got cut short because I got a call and had to rush back to the office. Come to think of it, though, it seemed like we were finished anyway. He was telling me to bring him a cashier's check when the phone rang, so I guess we were wrapping up."

"Well, you're in the clear then, so that's good. Let's do a little investigating before you make a final decision. Your money isn't going anywhere. Do you happen to remember the name of the fund he recommended to you?"

"No, but he gave me some information about it." Melissa reached into her bag and handed the brochure to Ben.

"Do you mind if I hang onto this for a day or two?" Ben asked. "I'll look into it and get back to you."

"Oh, sure, that's fine. I don't know what I'd do with it anyway. I don't want you to go to a lot of trouble, but I really appreciate your help, Mr. Guilford."

"It's no trouble at all, Melissa. I've made some good investment decisions and some bad ones, so you might as well benefit from my experience. Now who wants dessert? I can never pass up the crème brûlée here."

◆ ◆ ◆

Melissa was finishing up the design work on a client's new magazine ad when her office phone rang. She glanced at the caller ID window and the name Benjamin Guilford popped up.

"Hi, Mr. Guilford," she said into the receiver. "Thanks again for dinner last night. I had a really good time."

"You're more than welcome, Melissa." Ben said. "We enjoyed it too. Hey, I've been doing a little research on that mutual fund the broker recommended for you."

"Oh, thanks for doing that. What do you think?"

"I have some concerns about it, to tell you the truth."

"Okay . . . " This whole thing was not going anything like she'd expected.

"I don't know if you're aware of this, but most large brokerage houses like Morrow and Daniels are also in the business of managing investment products. It's a lucrative business for them because they earn a management fee as well as the commissions they get when one of their clients buys into those funds."

"Okay, I think I understand."

"As it turns out, Morrow and Daniels manages this particular fund. I didn't want to say anything last night because I didn't know for sure at the time, but that's what I was afraid of when you said this was Blackman's only recommendation, and that he started pushing you toward it without really working out an overall investment strategy with you first."

"So you're saying he and his firm would make a bigger profit if I put my money into this particular fund than another one that they didn't manage?"

"Exactly. This is why he has all those awards you saw in his office. He's a good salesman, and he knows which products earn his company the most money, so he pushes those first. Let me guess. I'll bet he had a pretty nice office, didn't he? Larger than a lot of his co-workers?"

"Well, I only saw a couple of others. His office was pretty close to the reception area, but yes, it was very nice."

"There you go," Ben said. "It works the same way in big law firms. The more money you bring into the firm, the better real estate you get to occupy."

Melissa was silent for a several seconds.

"Well, I really appreciate everything you've done, Mr. Guilford. I'm not feeling comfortable with Mr. Blackman anymore, so I don't think I'll go back to him, but this puts me back at square one. I've got no idea what to do with this money and now I'm feeling skeptical about finding the right financial advisor to help me. I don't want to get taken."

"I'll tell you what, Melissa. If you're comfortable, I'll make an appointment with a couple of different people, and I'll go with you to talk with them."

"Oh, I couldn't ask you to do that. You're really busy. I'll figure something out."

"It's really no trouble and I'd be happy to help you. Did Michael ever tell you about buying his first car?"

"No, I don't think so."

"We told him and his brother that if they saved half of the money for a decent used car, we would provide the other half. Michael got a job life guarding and he was pretty close to having enough for the car he wanted, and it happened that I was ready to trade in my car at about the same time. After I did my research and decided on the car I wanted, I took Michael with me to the dealership. I explained how the process usually worked, and I told him to pay close attention, because when it came time to buy his own car, I wanted him to negotiate for it himself. He sat there and listened while I went back and forth with the saleswoman, and in the end, we came to a satisfactory agreement on the car I wanted. That's how he learned."

"So Michael went by himself to buy his car? I can't imagine doing that as a teenager."

"No, I went with him, but that time I sat quietly and let him do the negotiating. It was fun watching him punch numbers into his calculator and stand up to the salesman's tactics. I was ready to step in if he needed help, but I didn't have to. He did it on his own."

"That's great," said Melissa, wondering what this had to do with her situation.

"Anyway, that's what I thought you and I would do. I'll make appointments with two or three people and we'll go together. At first I'll do most of the talking and you can learn the right questions to ask. Of course, you should feel free to speak up, but there won't be any pressure on you like there was in your meeting with Blackman. Then when you're comfortable, you can do the talking and I'll be there if you need me. How does that sound?"

"It sounds amazing," Melissa said, impressed that Ben was willing to spend so much time helping her. "I'd love to do that. Thank you so much."

"Not a problem. Let's look at our schedules and figure out some times when we're both available."

◆ ◆ ◆

The office of financial advisor Dan Burton was smaller than Perry Blackman's, and the view wasn't comparable, but Melissa felt confident as she took her seat. In the past week, she and Ben had met with three financial advisors and she had learned a great deal through the process.

The first one had been a stockbroker who, it turned out, had recently opened his own office after being let go from a mid-sized firm. Melissa had felt a little sorry for him because he was very anxious to please, but she agreed with Ben that he had neither the necessary credentials nor experience. She suspected that he'd be finding a new line of work within a year or so anyway.

The second was Janet Musto, a woman in her late thirties whose qualifications looked great. She'd spent the first five years of her career on Wall Street before returning to her native Chicago and joining a prestigious brokerage house there. She'd risen steadily and she had an impressive number of clients with even more impressive portfolios. Based on Ben's preliminary research, Melissa thought they'd found their ideal advisor . . . until they walked into her office.

The space itself was much like Blackman's had been. It was larger than those of her colleagues, beautifully appointed, and featured a spectacular view of the Navy Pier and Lake Michigan. That's where the similarities ended.

The place was a mess. The cleaning crew had vacuumed, emptied the trash, and otherwise done its job, but clearly they'd been able to save time on dusting because there wasn't a square inch of desk or table surface to be seen. The credenza behind Musto's desk was stacked with old copies of the Wall Street Journal, so many that throughout the interview, Melissa was distracted by worrying that they might come crashing down on top of her. Her printer's output tray was filled with sheets of paper and some had begun to cascade onto the floor. Next to the printer, her computer monitor showed a desktop screen with dozens of documents and spreadsheets scattered about rather than being organized into folders. Her desk was piled high with files, more newspapers, several legal pads and assorted paperwork. Apparently she'd recently bought a new cell phone, because the box, packing material and instructional manual were still on the desk. When Ben and Melissa arrived, Musto had to move another stack of files from one of the chairs opposite her desk so there would be room for both of them to sit down. She casually set the stack on the floor next to another.

"Sorry about the mess," she said a bit sheepishly. "Believe it or not, I do know what all this stuff is. I'm just so busy I can't seem to find time to put everything away. Once in a while, I come in on a Sunday afternoon and get everything organized. I guess it's time to do that again."

The meeting had gone smoothly except for a small hiccup when Musto had not been able to find the new box of business cards that had arrived the previous week. She scratched her name, phone number, and e-mail address onto a scrap of paper. "This will do in the meantime," she said.

"What did you think?" Ben asked as they left. He thought he could already tell by Melissa's demeanor, but wanted to hear what she'd say.

"She seems to have a great reputation and I liked her personally," she began. "It's just that . . . "

"It's okay, you can say it."

"I guess I'm kind of a neat freak and her office really bothered me. I don't think I'd feel confident that she could keep up with my investments if she can't keep up her office any better than that. If I called her about something, how would she find my information?"

"I couldn't agree more," Ben said. "We'll move on to the next one."

The third was a middle-aged woman named Karen Dunn who shared a suite of offices with seven other investment counselors. The meeting had started well, and Ben had seemed satisfied with the licenses and other credentials she held, but then things began to slide.

"Let me take this really quickly," she said when the phone rang. After a two-minute conversation with the client on the other end, she hung up and said, "I'll just be one more minute" before turning to her computer and spending a few moments typing.

"Sorry, I needed to complete a sale before the London market closed," she said. "Now where were we?"

By the time another 20 minutes had passed, Dunn had interrupted the meeting by taking two other calls, and after each one she had said the same thing—"Sorry. Now where were we?"

Ben ended the meeting shortly thereafter. In the elevator, he asked Melissa what she thought.

"She knows her business and has a lot of clients, but she seemed a little scattered to me," Melissa answered. "I can't put my finger on it, but something about her manner made me uncomfortable."

"Then that's all we need to know," Ben said. "I'm a believer in going with your instincts. If you don't have confidence in your doctor, you should find another one, and it's no different with your investment advisor. If something doesn't feel right, she's not the one for you."

Now, sitting across from Dan Burton, Melissa felt considerably more prepared than she had just a couple of weeks earlier when she'd met with Perry Blackman. After all the introductions had been made, Burton leaned forward with his arms on his desk, looked first at Ben and then at Melissa, and said, "Thanks for coming in today. What can I do for you?"

Ben glanced at Melissa, who opened the small notebook she was carrying and began speaking.

"I'm actually the client . . . or potential client, I guess. I'm looking for a financial advisor to help me invest some money I've inherited, and since I haven't done this before, Mr. Guilford is helping me."

"That's wonderful," Burton replied. "This can be a confusing business for a newcomer, so you're lucky to have someone with experience to give you a little guidance."

"I agree," Melissa said with a smile. "Now I've got some questions, if that's all right."

"Absolutely."

"First, can you tell me what kinds of financial licenses and ratings you have?"

Ben leaned back in his chair, pleased with Melissa's confidence. He had a feeling he wouldn't need to play much of a role here.

Burton's response was the one they were looking for. "I have series 7, series 24, and series 65 licenses," he said. "I'm legally authorized to deal in every type of investment—stocks, bonds, mutual funds, limited partnerships—as well as supervise other advisors. I've got a few other certifications as well. Here, let me give you a list." Reaching into a drawer, he pulled out a sheet of paper and handed it to Melissa.

Melissa consulted her notebook. Check, check, check.

The questions continued. Yes, his clients' accounts were covered by insurance. He'd been in business for 16 years. His firm managed accounts for more than 300 households, many of them having multiple accounts with the company. Neither he nor his practice had ever had a written complaint filed against them. He would be her primary contact, but someone else would be designated to answer her questions when he was out of the office. The firm offered regular educational seminars for its clients, and she would receive a monthly report on her investments.

Both Ben and Melissa studied Burton as he spoke. He answered all the questions with confidence and didn't seem annoyed by them, and he appeared to be in no hurry to move the meeting along. Finally Melissa came to the final question on her list.

"I have just one more question and it's one I hate asking. How do you earn your money? Do you take a commission or is it some other method?"

"Don't be embarrassed. It's a fair question," he said with a laugh. "I don't work on commission. I charge an annual fee based on the size of your account. I've found that method to be best for everyone, and I think it builds trust between my clients and me. They know I've got their best interests at heart. I'm not encouraging them to buy and sell securities so I can collect another commission, and I know that the size of my fee is determined by how well their investments are performing. If I do a good job at guiding you into the right investments, both of us make more money."

"That's exactly what I wanted to hear," Melissa said. "Believe it or not, you're the first financial advisor I've met who works that way."

"I hate to hear that, but it doesn't surprise me. Our business hasn't enjoyed the best reputation in the past few years, but I'm still proud of what I do. What else would you like to know?"

"That's all of my questions, actually."

"Well, let me know if you think of more. I like you, Melissa. Not many potential clients come so prepared. If we end up working together, essentially I'll be your employee, so you're smart to interview me before you hire me. Now, if you don't mind, I've got a few questions to ask you."

"Certainly."

"First, let me just tell you that my questions might seem personal, but I'm asking for a reason. My goal isn't to sell you a bunch of stocks or other investments to help you make money. What I do for my clients is protect what they already have first, and help them build wealth second. It might turn out that making investments isn't the best use of your money right now, and if that's the case, I'll tell you and we'll go from there."

"I understand."

The first question surprised Melissa. Burton wanted to know whether she was in good health and planned to continue working for the foreseeable future.

"That might sound like a strange question for someone your age, but I've got a client not much older than you who has a potentially debilitating illness," Burton said. "Our first goal is to plan for his medical care and make sure he'll be taken care of in the event that he's not able to work any longer."

"That makes sense."

More questions followed. Did she have a retirement plan? Did she have adequate insurance? Did she plan a major purchase such as a home or a new car in the near future? Was she in debt? Did she have long-term financial goals? He took plenty of notes and often referred to a checklist to be sure he wasn't forgetting anything.

The one question he didn't ask was how much money she had to invest. Melissa was amazed. For all he knew, her big inheritance could be $500.

As the conversation began to wind down, Burton sat back in his chair.

"Well, Melissa, I think I've got a pretty good picture of where you stand right now. What other questions do you have for me?"

"I can't think of anything else. I think we've covered just about everything . . . except how much money I have."

"Don't worry. I'm getting around to that! Here's how I typically work. Now that we've had a chance to get to know each other, why don't you go home and give it some thought? If you decide you want to work together, call me in the next day or so and we'll talk about the amount of money you have to work with. Then I'll come up with a plan and work the numbers, and we'll get back together to discuss it. How does that sound?"

Melissa paused for a moment and glanced at Ben. He gave her slight smile and nodded his head just a bit.

"No, that's all right, Mr. Burton. I don't need more time. My grandmother left me $20,000 and I'd like to hire you to help me make the most of it."

The Secret Explained: A Few Points to Remember

- When it comes to your money, your motto should be "safety first." Protect what you have.
- Don't take the word of anyone—a broker, other type of advisor, or potential business partner—that they're an expert who can be trusted. Investigate, verify, and verify again.
- Shyness doesn't pay. Ask plenty of questions before signing on with a financial expert. If you don't get the right answers, move on.
- Make sure you're diversified. What if all your eggs are in one basket, and you trip and fall?
- Trust your instincts. If something doesn't feel right—a broker, a specific investment—it isn't.
- Don't assume that an opulent office or an expensive suit is an indication of a financial advisor's professional ability.
- Get a clear understanding of how your advisor makes his money. Be sure you're not sacrificing your financial well-being to ensure his.

What's Your Skinny Cow?

- Are you intimidated by financial experts, making you afraid to ask questions or insist on a clear explanation of how and why your money is being invested?
- Do you assume that everyone with an office and an appropriate business card is a money master?
- Are you afraid to trust your instincts if something or someone just doesn't feel right?

Expense

Every money master knows one incontrovertible fact. Expenses can eat you alive and destroy your dreams of achieving wealth.

Some expenses are obvious—your mortgage, gas for your car, your morning latte. Others—the most dangerous—are the hidden ones like inflation and fees you might not even know you're paying.

In this chapter, we'll address both. We'll help you get a handle on what's coming in and going out, and then we'll tell you about some of those hidden expenses you might not be considering and can easily avoid once you're in the know. Pay attention because, for most of us, it's a lot harder to earn more money than it is to keep more of what we have.

The first step—the first *essential* step—to controlling your expenses is knowing what they are. That sounds elementary, doesn't it? In fact, it is elementary, but most people never take the time to track their expenses and find out exactly where their hard-earned money is going. It's one of the many simple money concepts that everyone is aware of, but few people actually put into practice.

To begin, get yourself a small notebook. For the next three months, you're going to keep track of every penny you spend, without fail. It sounds tedious (and it is!) but trust us, it will be worth the effort.

Start by keeping the receipt for every purchase you make, no matter how small and seemingly irrelevant. You might be surprised at how they add up at the end of the month.

This definitely includes the receipts for cash you withdraw from an ATM. It's astonishing how many people fail to log those withdrawals and find themselves facing an overdrawn checking account.

If you buy something for which you don't get a receipt, jot down the amount, along with a notation about what you purchased. At the end of each day, write down all of the day's expenses in your notebook. It only takes a few minutes, especially once it becomes a habit. At the end of the month, organize your expenses into categories—restaurant meals, gas, movies, and so on—to get a clear picture of how much money you're spending in each area of your life.

Next, set aside a Saturday to go back through your checking account records for the past year. Why a year? Because some expenses only come up annually, such as the membership fees for your automobile club and any organizations to which you belong. Perhaps you pay some bills quarterly, such as car insurance. Some expenses may fluctuate dramatically from one month to another. For instance, if you live in Texas, your utility bill is likely to be considerably higher during the hot summer months when the air conditioner runs constantly, and then drop off during mild winter months.

Here is a list of expenses to look for as you pull together your spending history. We've also organized the list into a handy worksheet on which you can keep track of your monthly expenses in each category and total them up for the year. You'll find the worksheet on our companion web site, www.the7secrets .net, and in Appendix B.

Home

Mortgage or rent	Home maintenance	Cleaning service
Property taxes	Homeowner's insurance	Pool/hot tub
Gas and electric		
Water	Security system	Land-line telephone
Cable/satellite TV	High speed Internet	Cell phone
	Other computer costs	

Food

Groceries	Alcohol	Restaurant meals
Tobacco		

Health

Medical insurance	Optometric insurance	Life insurance
Gym membership	Dental insurance	Veterinarian insurance

Transportation

Car payment	Car maintenance	Public transportation
Auto insurance	Parking	

Taxes, Loans, and Fees

Income taxes	Bank/ATM fees	Credit cards
Legal fees	Late fees	Loans
Accounting fees		

Personal

Clothing	Jewelry	Manicure/pedicure
Dry cleaning	Hair	Spa treatments

Children

Alimony/child support	School lunches	Sport fees
Tuition	Child care	

Entertainment

Books/magazines	Hobbies	Sporting events
Newspaper	Movies	Other

Miscellaneous

Lottery	Charitable donations	Other
Gifts	Vacations	

Now it's time to see how much money is coming in. Again, you'll find a worksheet in Appendix B and on our web site. In the meantime, following is a list of some of the ways in which you earn your income.

When you put it all together, were you surprised at what you learned? Are you spending $15 a month by using ATMs that charge a fee? Subscribing to magazines that you never read? Paying for a gym you use only rarely? Getting a true picture of how much money is going out, and exactly where it's going,

Income	Estimated Amount	Actual Amount
Paycheck (net)		
Social Security		
Pension		
IRA		
Disability		
Dividends from investments		
Rental income		
Fees		
Other		

is enormously freeing because it gives you an opportunity to change any spending habits that simply aren't working for you.

Most people who complete this exercise immediately see areas where they're spending more than they should. If that's the case with you, it's time to—you guessed it—develop a budget.

If you're unaccustomed to budgeting, it's not as intimidating as it sounds. Start by crossing off any fixed costs for which there is no wiggle room. These probably include your mortgage, car payment, and tuition for your children's schools. That should still leave plenty of categories in which you can cut back.

Begin by determining what is most important to you. If you're a dedicated exercise fanatic, you'll want to keep the gym membership, but perhaps you can cut back on restaurant meals. Can you use the public library rather than buying books and magazines? Vacation at a less expensive place? Spend an hour a week getting coupons from the newspaper or Internet to cut your grocery or take-out bills? Cut your own grass instead of paying for a lawn service?

After you've identified areas in which you're willing to cut back, decide exactly how much you want to spend on those items each month. Go to our web site for a worksheet to help you track your spending goals by category, as well as your actual costs.

Once you have a definite figure in mind for each expense category, it will be harder to let money slip through your fingers without ever realizing where it went. It takes discipline, but it's definitely do-able.

If self-discipline is a problem for you, learn to hold your own feet to the fire by using cash whenever possible. It's easier to spend more than you intended when you pay with a debit or credit card because it doesn't seem like you're actually spending money. That's not the case with cash.

Here's a way to make it easier. Let's say you've been treating yourself to too many restaurant lunches and you've decided to limit yourself to $50 a month in that category. At the beginning of the month, put $50 in cash into an envelope marked "Lunch." Use that money, and only that money, to pay for your lunch expenses, and when it's gone, it's gone. You can use the same tactic to limit your expenses in other areas like entertainment and clothing. If you have money left over at the end of the month, treat yourself to something, use it to stretch the next month's budget, or—here's a radical idea—save it!

If you're still having trouble mustering up the discipline to stick to a budget, think about what you could do with the money you'll save by cutting unnecessary expenses.

- Cutting out one $5 cup of gourmet coffee each week saves $260 a year.
- Cutting out two $15 pizzas a month saves $390 a year.
- Getting your nails done every two weeks instead of weekly saves $650 a year.
- Giving up a pack-a-day cigarette habit saves between $1,800 and $2,500 or more, in addition to the health benefits you'll achieve.

The True Cost of Credit Card Debt

If you're like most Americans, your expenses include monthly payments on credit cards. If you're not paying the full balance each month, then you need to understand how much those little plastic crutches are actually costing you, because of the miracle of compound interest.

If you're a saver, compound interest works in your favor because you earn returns on your original savings plus the interest that your money has earned so far. Suppose you put $100 into a savings account that pays 10 percent interest. (Yes, we know that's unheard of, but for the sake of simplicity, let's assume it's possible.) At the end of the first year, your account would be worth $110—your original $100 plus the $10 you earned in interest. The following year, your $110 would earn $11, leaving you with a total of $121. After 10 years, your original $100 would be worth nearly $260. Not too shabby!

Credit card debt works exactly like compound interest, with one small change. It favors the lender, not you. As your debt continues to accrue, you're paying interest on your interest. If your interest rate is 18 percent, your debt will double in just four years. In another four years, it doubles again, and so it continues indefinitely until you pay it off in full.

And make no mistake—your credit card company is extremely unlikely to ask you to pay off your balance. In fact, just the opposite is true. They very kindly allow you to make low monthly payments because that's how they make money— from the interest. You can continue to carry the debt indefinitely, paying ever-increasing amounts of interest each month.

No one benefits from credit card debt except the lender, so it makes sense that one of the best ways to reduce your expenses is by eliminating debt. Easier said than done? Maybe not.

While everyone agrees that debt elimination is necessary, there are several theories on the best way to accomplish it, particularly if you have several credit cards or other debts that continue to accrue interest.

Pay off the card with the highest interest rate first. This makes a lot of sense from a purely economic perspective because the interest is continuing to compound until the balance is paid off. The problem is that if the balance is a large one, it might be discouraging because it can take months or even years to pay it off.

Pay off the smallest debt first. Many people prefer this method because they see faster results and get a feeling of accomplishment as they see balances being eliminated. Once you've paid off one balance, apply that payment amount to the next smallest debt, and so on. For example, suppose you have three credit cards with balances of $1,200, $2,500, and $3,700. After paying all your other bills and the minimum balances of all three cards, you have $100 a month left over for your debt reduction program. Faithfully add that $100 to the minimum payment of card A, the one with the $1,200 balance, until it is completely paid off. Then apply the total payment you've been making on card A, including the extra $100, toward each month's payment on the $2,500 balance. You won't miss the money, your debts will be eliminated much faster, and you'll feel great each time you eliminate a debt entirely and have one less bill to pay.

Negotiate with your creditors. This makes many people uncomfortable, but it's a legitimate and often effective way to reduce your debt. Call your creditors, make sure you're speaking with someone authorized to make decisions, and ask for a reduction in interest or principle. Honesty is always the best policy. Explain that you're having financial difficulty and ask what they can do to help. You might also mention that you're considering filing for bankruptcy. Most creditors would prefer to work with you by lowering your interest rate rather than take a chance on having the debt wiped out by bankruptcy.

Contact a reputable debt consolidation company. A trained counselor will talk with you about your specific situation and design a plan tailored to your needs. Typically, these organizations are able to negotiate with your creditors for lower interest rates as long as you continue in the program, enabling you to pay your debts much faster than if you continued paying your current interest rates. There are several nonprofit debt consolidation organizations that charge a modest fee for their services.

Because we feel that debt reduction is such an essential part of building wealth, we have developed an amazing software product called The Money Grid that will enable you to take control of your finances and get completely out of debt— including your mortgage—in as little as seven years without changing your lifestyle. How does it work? By calculating all of your debts and determining the most efficient way to pay principle rather than interest.

Go to www.moneygridinternational.com to learn more about how The Money Grid can help you get out of debt as quickly as possible and begin to build wealth. To make it even easier, we're offering a seven-day free trial to readers of *The Seven Secrets of the Money Masters*. You'll find simple instructions for getting your free trial on the web site.

Not all expenses are as obvious as the ones we've looked at so far. In order to completely get a handle on your expenses, it's necessary to look for the hidden ones that most of us never consider.

Inflation

Inflation steals your money like a thief in the night. It creeps up quietly, inching its way into your bank account and robbing you blind.

Inflation is what happens when the cost of goods and services goes up, causing the value of your money to go down. It's calculated from the Consumer Price Index, and typically the rate goes up between 2.5 and 3.5 percent each year.

Let's look at an example in Table 3.1. Between 2005 and 2006, the inflation rate was 3.2 percent, so an item that cost $20 in 2005 cost $20.65 a year later. That's affordable, right? Look again. Suppose you spent $30,000 on goods and services in 2005. Just one year later, those same items would have cost $30,967.74—nearly $1,000 more.

Now let's stretch the example over a longer period. In 1960, a gallon of gas cost about 30 cents. Today, depending on where you live, it's tough to find it much under $3 a gallon. That's an inflation rate of nearly 1,000 percent in 40 years!

Obviously the average person's income has increased considerably over that same time period, but it certainly hasn't increased by 1,000 percent. While inflation isn't a direct expense that you can write a check for or put on a credit card, it can wreak havoc on your bottom line, so it's important to

Table 3.1: Prices from 1960 to 2009

	New Home	Gallon of Gas	Dozen Eggs	Gallon of Milk
1960	$ 16,500	$ .31	$ .57	$ .49
1970	$ 26,600	$ .36	$ .62	$1.15
1980	$ 76,400	$1.25	$ .91	$2.16
1990	$149,800	$1.16	$1.00	$2.78
2000	$207,000	$1.54	$ .89	$3.00
2009	$270,000	$2.34	$2.89	$3.39

look for ways to protect your financial position, not just today but over the next 20 or 30 years and beyond.

One possibility for hedging against inflation is attempting to lower the cost you pay for goods and services through negotiation. One of our favorite mantras is ABN—Always Be Negotiating.

All of us are accustomed to negotiating when we go into a dealer showroom to buy a car, or when we make an offer on a new home. In those businesses, it's customary and expected to offer less than the asking price and try to get a better deal, but most of us never think about bargaining to lower the cost of other expenses. There's nothing wrong with trying to negotiate a better deal as long as you're fair to the other party. It never hurts to ask, because the worst thing that can happen is that they will say no.

Another option is bartering—trading your own goods, skills, or services for something you need. We have a friend who is a talented graphic designer and equally talented at bartering. When she wanted a swing set and jungle gym for her children, she found an independent contractor who constructed wonderful playground sets and she offered him a deal, which he accepted. She designed and produced the marketing materials he needed to promote his fledgling business, in exchange for his building the swing set for her children. She has bartered with seamstresses, auto mechanics, and even the owner of a dog obedience school. Both parties reduce their expenses and everyone wins.

Fees on Investments

You make investments in order to earn money, but how much are those investments really costing you? Probably more than you realize.

Shockingly, regardless of your stock portfolio or mutual fund's performance, quarterly fees are taken directly from your account balance. During years when your portfolio is performing well, this might seem like money well spent. However, take a look at the NASDAQ from 2001 to 2003, the period known as the bursting of the dotcom bubble. If your holdings were weighted heavily in technology stocks, you might have lost 40 to 60 percent of your entire portfolio. Do you think your fees were reduced accordingly? We can assure you, they were not.

For many people, a 401(k) is their primary investment vehicle and the one they're counting on to carry them through retirement. What most of them don't realize is that a 401(k) comes with a whole host of fees—audit fees, administrative staff compensation fees, employee communication fees, non-mutual fund investment fees, record keeping fees, and compliance fees, just to name a few. Over the life of your 401(k) those fees really add up, and not in your favor. The laws of compound interest dictate that these small reductions in your total investment are magnified greatly over the decades in which many employees participate in such plans.

How about an example from *Forbes* magazine?

Over a lifetime of contributing $5,000 per year, assuming an annual gross rate of return of 9 percent, a participant paying an additional fee of just 1 percent would retire with $1,918,678 rather than $2,448,895. That's $530,217 less! That 1 percent difference in fees could wipe out 26 percent of the employee's retirement nest egg.

Reducing the fees that come with your investments is another reason to be very careful in choosing a financial advisor, and to be very sure you understand the investments he or she recommends before saying yes. Let's talk a little more about how brokers get paid.

Each time you buy or sell a stock, your broker gets a commission. The more often you turn over investments, the more commissions your broker earns, so it's easy to see why so many of them urge clients to buy and sell more often than might really be prudent.

But that direction might also be coming from the higher-ups in the brokerage firm. Typically, a broker receives 40 percent of the commission from buying or selling a stock, while the firm gets 60 percent. Most brokers are under enormous pressure to bring in as much money as possible, and often brokerage firms offer incentives to those who excel the most at improving the company's bottom line, or who push certain products that earn more money for the firm. If your broker has a plaque on his office wall touting his membership in the firm's Circle of Excellence or some other exclusive club, that doesn't mean his clients' portfolios are performing better than those of his colleagues. It means that your broker has outperformed his colleagues in terms of generating income for the firm. Does that sound like it's in your best interests?

We're not saying that your financial advisor doesn't want you to make money. Presumably, the more money you make from your investments, the happier you'll be and the more you'll continue to invest through the advisor. And there's also the other side of the coin. The more you invest, the more fees and commissions the advisor makes.

Commissions for buying and selling stocks are far from the only way your broker and the firm profit from your investments. Many people are surprised to learn that their financial advisor has put them into investments with large up-front commissions. When the entire commission is taken at the beginning of your investment, especially if it's a long-term one, you might want to consider how much incentive the broker now has to continue working for you. That's the point at which some people report that their phones calls are no longer being returned by their once-eager investment counselors.

A long-term investment can incur another potential expense if you find that you need to get out of that particular one. A surrender charge—a fee for selling or cancelling certain types of investments and annuities before they fully mature—can be as high as 20 percent of the investment's value. The maturity time can vary from one to 15 years, so unless you're absolutely certain you won't need to get out of an investment early, it's best to avoid those with up-front commissions and the resulting surrender charges. Instead, look for investments that will keep you more liquid and avoid tying up your funds for long periods of time.

Also bear in mind that it might be in the broker's best interest to sell products that benefit him or his employer rather than you, the client. Many banks and brokerage houses create or manage mutual funds and other investment products, and the more money is invested in those products, the more money the firm makes. Before agreeing to invest in a fund that your broker is recommending, find out whether it is tied to his firm in any way. Remember, it doesn't matter how great your advisor's jokes are or that he never fails to ask about your daughter's soccer team. He doesn't work for you. He works for himself and his firm, and their interests come first.

To avoid those inherent conflicts of interest, look for a financial advisor who earns her money through pay-as-you-go fees. These could be quarterly or annual fees, usually 1 percent or less depending on the size of your account and the effort involved, or even an hourly rate. She will have more incentive to continue working for you because she makes or loses money when you do.

Stocks and mutual funds aren't the only investments that come with built-in expenses. What about real estate? The mortgage on a piece of investment property is just the beginning. Taxes, repairs, maintenance, licenses, management costs, and more can eat away at your profits if you're not careful.

The key is to thoroughly investigate any investment—stocks, mutual funds, real estate, commodities—*before* handing over your money, in order to ensure that there are no surprises in terms of how much the investment is actually going to cost.

The Cost of Your Time

Clichés often become clichés because they're true, and that's certainly the case with the expression "time is money." How much is your time worth?

Some years ago, as Robert's real estate business was picking up steam, he continued to do his own accounting. By his own admission, he wasn't particularly good at it, but he felt that it was part of his role as the owner of the business. As the business grew, the accounting tasks came to eat up at least 30 hours a month. When he eventually broke down and hired a CPA to take care of the financials, he quickly saw that his bottom line increased rather than decreased. Why? Because a large chunk of his time had been freed to pursue new investments that brought more money into the company.

Andrew Carnegie, whom no one ever accused of being a slacker, summed it up when he said, "I'd rather have 1 percent of 100 people's efforts than 100 percent of my own." Think about how that might apply to your business and your life. Are there ways to set things up so you don't have to do everything yourself, ways that would free more of your time to pursue new wealth-building strategies?

In addition to the hours in a day, it's also important to look at what you're spending in mental, physical, emotional, and spiritual capital. If you're offered a job that would increase your income by 50 percent but would require you to spend 40 weeks of the year on the road, consider whether the additional income is worth the potential cost to your marriage, your family, and your spirit.

Tracking Your Time

The most important asset you have is your time. How are you using it? Start looking at how you're spending it and whether you could make changes that would benefit you financially and in terms of the overall quality of your life.

Just as you learned to track your expenses until you got a firm handle on them, make a habit of tracking your time.

- Make a note of each activity you've undertaken. Did you call clients? Read the newspaper? Chat with colleagues about last night's game? Make cold calls in an effort to generate sales?
- Write down how much time you spent on each activity.
- Did it make any money for you? Might it make money for you in the future?
- Consider whether you enjoyed the activity. If you get a knot in the pit of your stomach each time you have to make a sales call, maybe you're in the wrong business. Money masters know that life isn't just about building wealth.
- Can someone else do it? Are there things you can delegate to a subordinate in order to free more time for activities that would be more productive or lucrative? Might it be worthwhile to pay someone to do mundane things that eat up your day and give you less time for more lucrative or enjoyable activities?

Each week, set aside about 15 minutes to look at how you've spent your time. Friday afternoon is a good time to do this, because you're winding up the work week and can look ahead to the next one. Simply create the following type of spreadsheet and complete it every week. For your convenience, we have included this worksheet on our web site, www.the7secrets.net.

	Activity	Time	Money	Did You Enjoy?	Can Someone Else Do It?
1					
2					
3					
4					
5					

There's a good chance you'll find that you're spending a high percentage of your time on tasks that don't increase your wealth, could be done as well or better by someone else, and don't give you a sense of satisfaction or accomplishment.

Tracking your time doesn't take long, especially once you get into the habit of it, but it can pay huge dividends in terms of your finances and your lifestyle.

Lost Opportunities

Finally, let's consider the greatest expense of all—lost opportunities. If your money isn't working for you, what is that costing you? Possibly a lot.

Remember the miracle of compound interest? If everything you have is tied up in certificates of deposit that are only earning 2 percent interest at the most, you're missing out on opportunities to pursue the higher-yielding investments that are available out there. Over a period of 10, 20, or 30 years, the difference between earning 2 percent and 6 percent is enormous.

Next we'll talk about the other side of lost opportunity—the need for cash flow.

• • •

Michael's head was throbbing. He and his father had been working for more than two hours, and the headache seemed to get worse with each passing minute. He appreciated his father's willingness to help him find his way out of the financial mess he'd made, but going over every detail of his pitiful situation was beyond excruciating.

"I'll be back in a second, Dad," he said. "I'm going to get something for my headache. Do you want anything when I come back?"

"No, I'm fine," Ben replied without looking up from his calculator.

Michael took his pain tablets into the kitchen and pulled a can of soda from the refrigerator. He walked over to the door and looked out onto the patio. It was a perfect spring day—sunny, warm, breezy. He glanced at his watch. 3:45. His buddies were playing basketball at the park right now. He idly considered slipping quietly out the door and going to join them. He laughed quietly. He had tried sneaking out of the house a few times when he was a teenager. It had never worked well for him, so it was doubtful that this time would turn out any better.

He returned to the dining room to find that his father had disappeared. Michael followed the sound of clicking computer keys into Ben's home office, where his father was busily tapping on the keyboard.

"Are we finished for today?" Michael asked, trying not to sound too hopeful.

"No, just give me a minute. I'll be right with you," Ben replied. Michael's hopes of catching up with his friends faded quickly.

Ben returned to the dining room shortly, carrying a sheet of paper and what appeared to be a small notebook.

"Okay then," Ben began. "We've gone over your bank account pretty thoroughly and it's clear that you're hemorrhaging money, but what isn't clear is exactly where it's going."

"Yeah, I know," Michael said. "I take money out at the ATM and a couple of days later it's gone and I go back for more. I don't feel like I spend a lot, but if I didn't, I guess I wouldn't be broke, right?"

"Exactly, so the first thing we have to do is find out where all that money is going. Here, I've got a couple of things for you."

He pushed the notebook across the table toward Michael. It was a garden-variety booklet from an office supply store with the word "Expenses" stamped across the front. It was filled with lined pages containing four columns: Date, Expenditure, Amount, and Tax. In the back was a small pocket. Michael could see where this was going.

"I want you to carry this with you from now on and write down every dime you spend," Ben said. "I got one small enough to fit into your pocket, so there's no excuse for not having it with you." His father knew Michael a little too well.

"Every dime? Isn't that going a little bit overboard?" Michael asked.

"Look, you don't have to do it forever. Just do it for a couple of months until you find out where the holes in your pockets are. I'll bet you'll be surprised at how much you're spending without even thinking about it. You'll have it right there in your pocket, and I know you always carry a pen, so it will just take a couple of seconds."

"Okay, I guess I could do that," Michael said somewhat grudgingly. Less than a week ago, his father had bailed him out by writing a pretty big check. He supposed the least he could do was humor him with this little project.

"As you can see, there are spaces for the date, what you spent the money on, and the amount. The 'tax' column is for expenses that are tax deductible. Just put a check in it if that applies, and put the receipt into the little pocket in the back. That way, you'll have everything ready when tax time comes."

"That makes sense," Michael replied. Even though he was an accountant, he often scrambled to gather all the pertinent information when he was ready to prepare his tax returns.

"And another thing," Ben said. "I also want you to write down when you take cash from the ATM, and put the receipt for that in the pocket too."

"Why? I'm already going to be writing down what I spend it on."

"I know, but I think it would help you get a handle on how much cash you're withdrawing every week. You remember how long it took me to start using ATMs. I was a technophobe back then, but it was more than that. It just seemed too easy. I was afraid I'd lose track of what I had in my account, and I'm guessing that's been happening to you since you've been getting overdrawn."

"I guess that's true. I usually glance at the slip to see what my balance is, but if I'm in a hurry, I don't even do that."

"You also need to keep those receipts in case there's ever a question about your account," Ben said. "Without a receipt, you've got no proof that you took out $50 if the bank says you withdrew $500. It's the same with receipts for things you buy with your credit or debit cards. If someone makes a mistake or hacks into your account, you need proof."

"Okay, that's a good point. That's never happened to me, but I guess it's always a possibility."

"Good. Then when you come over here on Sunday, we'll go over your expenses together and put them into categories. That's what these charts are for," Ben said with a smile as he produced two sheets of paper. Creating tables and charts on his computer was a recently-developed skill and he was extraordinarily proud of the accomplishment.

Michael glanced at the page. Running down the left side was a list of expenses—everything from his mortgage and utilities to movie rentals and shoe shines.

"We'll sort your expenses into these categories and add them up. I left some lines blank in case there are categories I didn't think of. At the end of the month, we'll put it all together and then we'll have a clear idea of where your money is going and where you might be able to cut back."

"Why don't we just wait until the end of the month and do it all at once?"

"You can do that eventually, but right now, do you really want to wait another four weeks to start getting this thing under control?"

"Good point. Okay, I'll start tomorrow."

"What's wrong with today?"

◆ ◆ ◆

Over the next week, Michael attacked his new project with mixed results. On Monday, he was running late, forgot to put the notebook in his pocket, and only remembered when he stopped for coffee at the kiosk in the lobby of his office building.

"Hey, could I get a receipt for that?" he asked.

The cashier shrugged.

"Sure, just a second." Who needed a receipt for coffee and a bagel?

On Tuesday, he remembered the notebook and dutifully recorded the gas he bought on the way to work, his coffee and bagel, and the lunch he had delivered to his office. He was feeling pretty proud of himself until he handed over his debit card to pay for drinks at his regular Tuesday night happy hour. Michael thought about reaching for the notebook, but decided against it. There was no reason his friends had to know that his father had assigned him a belt-tightening project. When the waitress returned with his receipt, he jotted down the amount of his tip and put the receipt in his pocket. He would record it when he got home, he told himself.

By Saturday, recording his expenses has become almost routine. Without thinking, he even brought out the notebook to record the movie tickets he bought that night.

"What are you writing down?" Melissa asked.

"Oh," Michael said hesitantly. Maybe he could pass this off without bringing in his "Sundays with Dad" meetings and the humiliating experience that had led to them. "I'm trying to keep track of the money I spend so I can get a better handle on my finances," he said, hoping he sounded casual. "Now that you're an heiress, I've got to try to keep up." He gave her his best teasing smile.

"That's not a bad idea. Maybe I should do that too," Melissa replied.

◆ ◆ ◆

The next day, Michael glanced through the little notebook as he waited for his father to get off the phone and join him. Reaching for the worksheet Ben had made, he pulled a pen out of his pocket. Might as well get started.

The first entry was the pizza he'd ordered for dinner the previous Sunday night. The sum of $14.29 went into the food category.

Next came Monday morning's coffee and bagel. He recorded $9.47 in the same column. Lunch had cost $12.38 and the drive-through fast food that had been his dinner was $7.46. He was running out of space in that column and he hadn't even come to Tuesday yet.

Ben came into the room a few minutes later to find his son hunched over the table, hard at work.

"How's it going?"

"Oh, hey, Dad. Okay, I guess. You're right, it's pretty eye-opening."

"In what way?"

"Well, for example, so far I've got more than $160 in food and I'm only up to Friday morning. Melissa and I went out last night and the bill was over $80 for that meal alone."

"Did you realize you were spending that much?"

"No, I had no idea. Apparently I spend $50 a week just on coffee and a bagel on my way to work every day. It doesn't seem like that much when you look at it one day at a time, but it adds up."

"It sure does. I thought this might be a wake-up call, but I'm a little surprised you're getting the picture so soon."

"Numbers don't lie, I guess."

"No, they don't. Let's see what else you've got there."

Twenty minutes later, the week's expenses had been tallied. Michael looked glumly at the page in front of him. He'd spent almost $300 on food, most of it for take-out or meals he'd eaten in restaurants. There was $27 for parking in garages other than his own, $13 for some sports magazines he's picked up at a bookstore, and $22 for the movie he and Melissa had seen, plus another $14 for snacks and drinks. He'd paid his cable and Internet bills, gotten two suits dry cleaned and five shirts laundered, bought a new pair of running shoes, and gotten a haircut. He'd repaid his friend Tim for his ticket to next week's Cubs game and chipped in on birthday flowers and lunch for his department's administrative assistant. When he saw the grand total, his chest felt tight as he visualized his paycheck and did the mental math. He'd spent more than he'd earned that week. Again.

Ben studied his son carefully. "What do you think?"

Michael leaned back and ran his hands through his hair. "I think I know why I'm in trouble."

"Good. Now let's figure out what to do about it."

By the time Michael picked up his paperwork and headed home, the two men had figured out several ways for cutting back on his expenses. Eating breakfast at home would save about $30 even if he still picked up a cup of regular coffee at the lobby kiosk. He could cut his parking expenses by walking or taking a taxi to meetings that took place just a few blocks from his office. The magazines still sat unread on his coffee table, so maybe next time he'd think twice about how much he needed them. He still wanted to go to nice places with Melissa, and he would never pass up a chance at Cubs tickets, but those things would be more affordable if he cut back on some of the less important expenses.

As he walked Michael to the door, Ben had cautioned him to continue recording and monitoring his expenses.

"This is just one week," he'd said. "Next week might be entirely different. You've got to keep at this vigilantly until you've got things under control. Do you still watch the Discovery Channel?"

"You know I'd never miss Shark Week."

"Right! A few months ago, I was watching a series on space exploration and they said something that stuck with me. Apparently a rocket heading to the moon is off course something like 97 percent of the time."

"How can that be? They never miss the mark."

"Exactly. It's because they have a system of checks and they're constantly making small adjustments and corrections. That ensures that they never veer too far off course and even when they do veer off a little, they get right back on track. That's what you need to do with your finances. Give yourself a weekly check-up so you can make a correction if you're starting to get off course."

The next morning, the coffee kiosk attendant automatically reached for a bagel when she saw Michael approaching.

"Nope, not today," he said, holding up his hand in a "stop" motion. "Just regular coffee please. I've already eaten."

◆ ◆ ◆

Sunday afternoon rolled around faster than Michael expected and he drove to his parents' home filled with dread. He didn't look forward to sharing his out-of-control everyday expenses with his father, but that was nothing compared to what he was about to face. Today the topic was credit cards.

Michael remembered his first experience with credit cards in painful detail. He was enrolled as a freshman at the University of Michigan. His parents drove him to Ann Arbor and helped him get settled in his dorm room. The next two days were a whirlwind of orientation and learning his way around the large campus. He found himself inside the book store, clutching the lengthy list of books he needed for his first semester of classes. As he made his way through the crowded aisles, checking off his list as he picked up the thick volumes, he was aware that the cost was getting high, but he wasn't concerned. His parents knew how expensive college textbooks were, especially if you couldn't find used ones, so they gave him an ample amount of cash for books and other living expenses, along with strict orders to open a checking account as soon as possible. He was so busy that he hadn't done it yet, but it wasn't a problem. He would just pay cash for the books.

After what seemed like hours of shoving his way from humanities to accounting to biology and American history, Michael joined the long line at one of the cash registers. His arms ached from the heavy load of the books. This was going to take forever.

"Hey, those look heavy." He turned to see three pretty girls sitting at a long table. The blonde was looking at him and smiling. Was she talking to him?

"Yeah, they are." Lame, he thought. So lame.

"You can set them here if you want," the blonde said. "We're giving away free t-shirts. Would you like one?"

He glanced at the person ahead of him. The line was beginning to inch forward. If he went over to the table, he would lose his place and have to start over. If he stayed in line, he would be passing up a chance to meet a pretty girl and get a free t-shirt. No contest.

Michael walked the few feet to the table and gratefully set his books on the corner.

"Thanks," he said. "I'm Michael, by the way."

"Hi, Michael. I'm Mandy." He bet she spelled it with an i on the end. They were going to have really beautiful children.

"So why are you giving away t-shirts?"

"We work for Citibank. They want to introduce themselves to new students and see how they can help you," Mandy said, gesturing toward the other two girls. Both of them were chatting away with guys who looked very much like him, all with big stacks of heavy books that now rested on the table.

"Well, as it happens, I'm looking for a bank," Michael said. "I need to open a checking account, but I've been too busy so far. Maybe I'll check them out."

"You definitely should," Mandy replied, handing him a neatly folded t-shirt. "They've got great services. As a matter of fact . . . did you say you haven't opened an account yet?"

"Yeah, I'm going to try to get to it tomorrow."

"So are you paying cash for your books?"

"Yeah."

She eyed the stack and raised her eyebrows, then pressed her lips together and looked back at Michael.

"I know of a way that you could get all your books and keep the cash. That money would buy a lot of pizza."

Michael hesitated. How was that possible? And more important, was she hinting that she'd go for pizza with him?

"Okay, tell me."

Mandy picked up a brochure and handed it to him. The brochures were obscured by the tall stack of t-shirts. He hadn't even seen them.

"Citibank is offering credit cards to new students. There's an introductory rate of 0 percent interest for the first three months, and if you qualify, you can get instant approval from my boss over there." She tilted her head toward a man in a bright blue Citibank golf shirt seated at the end of the table. "I'm sure you'll qualify," she said with a charming smile.

Michael briefly wondered what his parents would say about this. As soon as he turned 18, he began to get credit card offers in the mail, but his parents had put them into the shredder without opening them. "It's too easy to get sucked into that whole culture of debt, and you're just not responsible enough to handle it yet," his mother had said.

But this was different. No interest for three months? What could be wrong with that? He'd charge his textbooks, put the cash into the bank, and pay the bill when it came. His parents would be proud that he'd gotten such a great deal. And in his first week of school!

Within 15 minutes, Michael was back at the end of the line, shifting the weight of his books from one arm to the other to relieve the ache in his forearms. Tucked into the top book was his credit card application, stamped and signed by the man in the blue golf shirt, signifying that he, Michael W. Guilford, was a customer in good standing with Citibank and that he could charge up to $4,000. He glanced back at Mandy, who was smiling broadly at a tall, dark-haired guy as she handed him a t-shirt.

The outcome of his relationship with his shiny new Citibank credit card was not nearly as pleasant as the beginning. By the time his introductory period ended, his balance reached $429.45. With the new 12 percent interest rate, the total was just over $480. He was a little short that month, so he paid the minimum allowed and vowed to pay the rest off soon. The following month, he only used the card three times, but somehow when the bill arrived it was $554.38. What?

When Christmas shopping took the balance to more than $850, he panicked and put the card into his dresser drawer, but pulled it back out two months later. He wasn't about to miss spring break in Cancun, even though his bank account was low again. He charged the plane ticket and his share of the hotel room and used his cash for food and other expenses.

By the time he arrived home for summer break, Michael knew he was in trouble. He had a summer job lined up, but it didn't pay much and his car insurance was due. His parents had given him permission to take his car back to campus in the fall, so he would have to add gas and maintenance to his regular expenses, which already were more than he'd anticipated.

His parents were surprisingly understanding about it. They administered the lecture he anticipated, paid off his balance, and watched as he called Citibank to cancel the account. Then they put his card into the shredder.

He hadn't even got a date with Mandy out of it. The number she wrote on the palm of his hand turned out to be the university's French Department.

◆ ◆ ◆

Walking through his parents' kitchen door, Michael couldn't believe he was in the same situation again. He walked the straight and narrow during his last three years in Ann Arbor, but when he returned to Chicago and started a job, the credit card offers came pouring in again. He signed up for one, thinking he would need it for car rentals and shopping online. Then he got another card because the company was giving a free five-day trip to Florida to new customers. He didn't even remember what his rationale was for getting the third one, but he felt exactly like he felt the day he confessed the Citibank debacle to his parents. Worse, really. That bill had been less than $2,000. The total he now owed was more than ten times that amount.

Ben was seated at the kitchen table. He looked up from the Sunday sports section when Michael entered.

"What's wrong with you? You look as guilty as sin. You didn't break the Crawfords' window with a baseball again, did you?"

"No, sir," Michael said with a slight smile. He slumped into a chair across from his father and set a manila folder on the table.

"If you're calling me 'sir,' something's up."

Michael sighed. "I'm just embarrassed, I guess. You thought I'd learned my lesson after I got into credit card trouble in college, and I thought so too, but now here I am again and it's worse than ever. A lot worse."

"Oh, right. The blonde with the t-shirts. What was her name? Cindy?"

"Mandy."

"Mandy. That's right. That was the most expensive t-shirt I ever bought."

"I'll bet," Michael replied with a laugh. At least the mood was lightening a little.

"Well, we might as well get to it. Show me the damage," Ben said as he put his reading glasses back on.

The balances on the three cards totaled $21,386.75.

Ben didn't say anything, but gave Michael a look that spoke volumes.

"I don't know exactly how it happened," Michael said in response. "When I bought the condo, I needed furniture. My apartment was a lot smaller, so there were things I didn't have, and I just . . . wanted better stuff, I guess."

"That's understandable."

"Then . . . I don't know. I had some car repairs. Sometimes I'd charge dinner or clothes. Oh, the vacation to Hawaii, and Brad's bachelor party weekend in Vegas. I guess it was just a little here and a little there, until a little became a lot. Then I had to stop charging things because all my cards were pretty much maxed out, and I suppose that's when I started getting into trouble with my checking account."

"You became used to spending more than you had because you were able to charge things, and your spending habits didn't change when charging wasn't an option anymore."

"Exactly."

"Right," Ben said. "Well, it's a lot, but let's see what we can do."

He spread the three bills side-by-side on the table and studied them, then shuffled the order. Taking a legal pad and a pen, he drew a makeshift chart. In one column, he wrote the name of the lender and the balance on each card. In the second column, he noted the interest rate, and in the third the minimum balance Michael owed on his current statements. He looked at the list and smiled.

"Citicard again? Really?"

"They gave me a free trip to Florida," Michael said sheepishly.

Ben shook his head and looked back at the chart. He turned it around so Michael could see it.

"Here is who you owe, what you owe, and how much it's costing you to owe this money. I've listed the three cards in the order of the interest rate, from lowest to highest. There are a couple of ways to do this, but I think you should pay off the one with the lowest interest rate first. I know how you think, and it would help if you could see progress sooner rather than later."

"That's the problem, Dad," Michael said, standing up and pacing the floor in frustration. "I can't pay them off. I can barely pay the minimum every month. It's impossible."

"Settle down. Listen to what I'm suggesting before you get upset. You're still in the process of trying to get your spending under control, so I understand that you don't have extra money to put toward paying off your debts right now. That's why I'm going to help you for a while to get you started."

Michael sat back down. This was unexpected.

"Here's what we're going to do," Ben continued. "You're going to continue paying the minimum each month on the MasterCard and VISA bills, but I'm going to give you $200 to add to your Discover bill."

"Dad, you don't have to do that . . ."

"Oh, don't worry, I'm not going to do it forever. Just like those low introductory rates, this offer is only good for three months. By that time, I expect you to have established a budget that will enable you to live within your means—actually, *below* your means so you'll have money left over instead of coming up short every month. Then you'll start contributing the extra $200 yourself. In fact, I hope you'll find even more that you can put toward paying this down. And by then, you'll have seen your principle go down by more than $600, and that will have caused the minimum payment to start inching down. You'll be surprised at how quickly you'll see progress . . . and how good it will feel."

"Okay, that sounds reasonable. But in the meantime, I won't be making progress on the other cards. Wouldn't it make more sense to divide the extra $200 among all three of them?"

"You could do that, but I think my way makes more sense. I haven't done the math, but at a glance, I'm estimating you'll have this first card paid off in about five months. Then you'll take all the money you've been sending to Discover and apply it to your VISA bill every month. See where I'm going?"

"Yeah, I do. It's kind of like a snowball effect."

"That's exactly what it's called. When the VISA balance is paid, you should have a pretty hefty sum to send to the good people at MasterCard every month, and before you know it, you'll be out of credit card debt. I figure it will take about three and a half years."

"Yeah, but if I could find even more than that initial $200, it would go even faster," Michael said. This was starting to sound kind of exciting.

"That's the way to think," Ben said as he put the bills back into the folder. "I'll get you the check for the first $200 while you see if there's any of your mother's coconut pie left in the refrigerator. I'm hungry."

The Secret Explained: A Few Points to Remember

- Begin immediately to track your income and expenses. It's impossible to get a handle on your personal or business finances unless you know how much is coming in, how much is going out, and where it's going.
- Develop a reasonable budget and stick to it.
- Get out of debt, especially credit card debt. No one is benefitting except your creditors.
- Be aware of hidden expenses, such as fees on your investments.

What's Your Skinny Cow?

- Do you spend money without thinking about it, often on things that aren't really important to you?
- Do you automatically reach for a credit card to pay for things you could pay for with cash?
- Do you waste your time on tasks that could be done faster and easier by someone else?

The 7 S.E.C.R.E.T.S

SECRET 3

Cash Flow

In today's economic environment, cash is absolutely king because, let's face it, you can't eat equity. In business and in your personal life, having sufficient liquid assets to cover emergencies and grasp opportunities when they arise can mean the difference between wealth and bankruptcy.

Cash flow is a fairly simple concept. It's how money flows in and out of your life or your business. It's simple, but it's also one of the primary reasons that businesses and people fail financially. Money masters know that no matter how wealthy someone appears to be on paper, real wealth is only possible with access to sufficient cash.

We've all heard the term "paper millionaire." It refers to someone who has a high net worth as a result of the total market value of the assets he or she owns. Typically this occurs when an investor buys marketable securities that increase dramatically in value. The catch is that, while the numbers look good on paper, the investments aren't really worth anything until they're liquidated, whereas a true millionaire is someone who actually has $1 million in cash.

There's a big difference, and it's a lesson that many people learned during the dot-com boom and subsequent bust in the late 1990s and early 2000s. Some investors became paper millionaires very quickly when their super-hot technology stocks went through the roof. The statement from the broker showed a net worth in the millions, and those investors became the darlings of Wall Street and the financial media. They were money masters. Or were they?

The ones who sold those technology stocks at the right time are real millionaires today. Those who didn't were left holding stacks of paper in the form of stock certificates that were essentially worthless. It was a classic example of easy come, easy go.

For businesses, having ample cash on hand is crucial to ensuring that employees and creditors will be paid on time, benefits plans will be funded, and the business can continue to operate seamlessly. Market analysts and investors also use cash flow as a measure of the company's financial performance, because cash-strapped businesses are not able to invest back into the company to generate growth and increase profits. When cash dries up, insolvency, liquidation of assets, and even bankruptcy often follow.

Did you know that even in the best of times, 20 percent of new businesses fail within the first two years of operation? Do you know why? It's not because the idea was a bad one. Almost every time a new business fails, it's because of cash flow issues.

And the problem isn't always a lack of customers. In fact, just the opposite can be true. If the demand for a business's products or services escalates dramatically, the owner needs to have enough cash available to buy more inventory or step up production. Let's look at a real life example.

Several years ago, an acquaintance of ours opened a new business buying and selling used college textbooks on line. Sam was young, bright, and eager, and he'd developed a business plan that looked solid.

Things got off to a good start and he started making a profit right away. Then he had a terrific idea. That social media phenomenon known as Facebook was getting increasingly popular, and Sam was one of the first people to use it as a marketing tool for his business.

At that time, Facebook was still being used primarily by college students and, of course, that was Sam's target market. He built a sizeable following as word spread that students could buy books from his web site at a lower price than even the discounted bookstores in many college towns.

Sam soon found himself with no shortage of customers who wanted to buy used textbooks from him and those who had books to sell. He was, however, short on one important thing—the cash he needed to maintain a sufficient inventory. Demand had exceeded supply, and he couldn't afford to do what was necessary to meet that increased demand.

You can guess what happened next. His customers were forced to go elsewhere, and Sam eventually was forced to shut the business down because his cash flow was inadequate.

Oddly enough, until shortly before his business went under, Sam was making a profit—a small one, but a profit nonetheless—which brings up another point. Don't confuse cash flow with profit. They're not the same thing.

A business is profitable if its revenue exceeds the amount of money it takes to run it. But if the company is not able to meet its obligations, it faces insolvency and, as Sam learned, those obligations can be more than paying for taxes, overhead, and other common expenses. Without the cash necessary to stock his inventory, he was out of business.

Robert had a similar experience a few years ago. While his business survived, it was a close call and taught him not to underestimate the importance of cash flow.

Robert owned more than 100 rental properties in Nashville when a tornado ripped through the area, destroying or seriously damaging nearly half of them. Fortunately, he had insurance and more than enough cash to rebuild the properties, or so he thought.

He hired construction crews to begin work within a day, and the tab for the first week's work was $80,000. While the insurance company continued to assure him that a check was forthcoming, two more weeks of $70,000-plus construction expenses wiped out every bit of cash he had in both his business and personal accounts.

A short-term bank loan bailed him out until the insurance money arrived, but it was a lesson well learned. The bigger the potential loss, the bigger your cash reserve needs to be.

Your Personal Cash Flow

We've seen how cash flow can make or break a business, but it's equally important in our personal finances. Cash flow issues can affect everything from your ability to pay your cable bill on time to actually losing your home.

Remember our first secret, safety? Money masters know that having access to adequate cash is key to maintaining the safety of what we already have. Being rich on paper doesn't mean much if you can't get to your money when you need it.

Many people believe they're being forward thinkers by putting everything they have into long term investments, but what happens if an emergency strikes? Job loss, a lengthy illness, a lawsuit, or any one of life's unexpected twists and turns can wipe out a savings account in a hurry, forcing you to begin selling off assets to survive.

And liquidating those assets isn't always easy. Real estate can be a great investment vehicle, but you have to be in it for the long haul. It can take months or even years to find a buyer for real estate, and depending on the current market and your level of desperation, you could easily end up taking a major loss. If you don't believe us, ask any of the thousands of people who have made the difficult decision to short-sell their homes, giving the lender an agreed-upon amount that is less than the amount owed, in order to avoid foreclosure.

Stocks are no better. The market has no sympathy for your personal economic crisis. If the price of your holdings is low at the time you're forced to sell in order to raise cash, Wall Street won't even send you a card, and someone with cash on hand will pick up your stocks at a bargain basement price.

What about other investments? Some, such as certificates of deposit, can be cashed in whenever you want, but there's a catch. Many carry stiff penalties for early withdrawal, and it's not uncommon for financial advisors to fail to mention this drawback when they're recommending such investments.

The Other Side of the Coin

Not only is cash flow necessary to save you or your business from financial ruin if things take a downward turn, it also gives you the ability to increase your wealth.

Having access to an adequate amount of cash enables you to strike while the iron is hot, taking advantage of low-priced stocks and other investment opportunities that those without liquid assets miss out on. When the market goes down, the people with the biggest smiles are those with enough cash and savvy to scoop up undervalued stocks, knowing that their value will increase soon.

Experienced real estate investors know this, too. In today's market, properties can be bought for cents on the dollar, but because lenders have clamped down on issuing credit, investors with cash are the ones who will come out on top in the long run.

Let's look at some statistics. Across the United States, housing prices fell an average of 13 percent between 2007 and 2009. That was very bad news for anyone trying to sell a home or a piece of rental property.

On the other hand, it was very good news for people with enough ready cash to purchase their dream home or a piece of investment real estate at a price that might not come around again for many years. In many U.S. communities, a family could have purchased a $300,000 home for $261,000—if they had access to the necessary funds and the foresight to seize the opportunity.

How Much Is Enough?

Two of the biggest mistakes we've seen people make with regard to cash flow are underestimating how much cash they need, and overestimating how much will be coming in.

If you've done the exercise in Chapter 3 to determine what your income and expenses really are, you know how much money you need each month to continue living your current lifestyle. Hopefully, your income is providing that amount and more. But what if your income stops? What if you decide to retire? What if you lose your job?

Every evening newscast seems to issue new reports about the nation's dire unemployment rate. Things of zero probability really do occur, and now even teachers and nurses—careers once thought to be recession-proof—are losing their jobs, so don't think for a moment that it couldn't happen to you.

Financial experts vary widely in their recommendations as to how much cash you should have on hand in order to survive the loss of your job. At the time of this writing, the U.S.

Bureau of Labor Statistics was reporting that four of every ten unemployed people had been jobless for more than 27 weeks, and that figure had remained unchanged for many months. That's six months, folks.

When the economy is strong, unemployment is low, and your particular industry is hiring rather than firing, it might be possible to squeak by with a three-month cash cushion to hedge against the unthinkable. Today, it's foolhardy to have less than six to nine months of living expenses in a money market account you can access whenever you need to.

Where should you keep your cash reserve? One of the best places to park it is in a money market account. They pay a bit more interest than standard savings accounts, but unlike certificates of deposit, they allow you to withdraw funds at any time with no fees or penalty.

You can open a money market account at your current bank, but it pays to take a little time to look around for the best interest rate. The web site www.bankrate.com is a good place to find out which banks are offering the best rates right now.

You might be surprised to find that the highest rates are being paid by banks that operate only over the Internet. Don't let that deter you from investigating further. As long as a bank is FDIC insured and meets all federal regulations, your money should be as safe with an online institution as it would be with the bricks-and-mortar bank down the street.

Of course, if it's important to you to be able to walk into a bank building and speak to a human being, you might be more comfortable maintaining a checking account at a local bank, but don't discount the possibility of using an Internet bank for the bulk of your savings. The difference between the interest rates paid by different institutions for the same type of accounts can be up to three percentage points, so it's foolish to give up that extra earning power.

Suppose you're putting $200 a month into a savings account to build up your cash reserve. In an account paying 2 percent interest, you'd have $26,543 after ten years. If you put the same amount of money into an account paying 4 percent interest, your balance would be $29,449 at the end of ten years. Quite a difference!

Even in the best money market account, your cash won't earn the same rate of return you could get with other investments. It also won't leave you rich on paper but having no money for groceries or gas.

• • •

Michael and two friends sat at their usual table at Butch McGuire's, sipping foamy pints of Guinness and talking about the fielder's error that resulted in a Cubs victory the previous night. These friends met at the Division Street pub after work every Tuesday for the past three years, a tradition they assumed would go on for the rest of their lives.

"Where's Brad?" Michael said, looking expectantly toward the door of the bar. "Did he say he wasn't coming?"

"No, I got a text from him as I was walking over here from work. He said something had come up and he'd be late, but that was it," Todd replied.

When Brad entered the bar and took his seat at the table a few minutes later, his facial muscles were tight and he looked distressed.

"Hey, about time you got here," Michael said. "Everything all right?"

Brad paused for a moment, glancing at his friends around the table. Might as well say it. They would find out sooner or later.

"No, not all right at all. I got laid off."

"*What?*" The question came in unison, as if they had rehearsed it.

"I don't get it," Michael said. I thought things were going great with your job."

"Apparently I was doing fine. My boss went on and on about how happy the company was with me, what a great loss this would be for them, blah blah blah. But the bottom line is that the economy is awful and construction is suffering as much or more than any other industry. The company doesn't need as many architects now and someone had to go. You know the rule—last hired, first fired—and that was me. Well, me and another guy, plus some people in other departments. I think there were 11 altogether."

"That's awful, man," Nick said, giving Brad a comforting pat on the shoulder. "I feel terrible for you. What did Emily say?"

"I haven't told her yet," Brad replied. "It just happened a couple of hours ago. I didn't want to tell her on the phone, obviously. She planned on having dinner with her sister tonight anyway, so I thought I'd come have a couple of beers with you guys, then I'll tell her when I get home."

"I'm sure she'll understand" Michael said. "It's not like it's your fault, and you'll find something else soon. Like your boss said, you're good at your job. It's just the luck of the draw."

"Oh yeah, I know, but she'll still be upset. The baby is due in less than four months and we hadn't planned for her to go back to work afterward, at least not for a year or so. Now . . . I don't know."

"I'm sure it will be fine," Todd said. "Besides, you've got money in the bank, right? You can float for a while."

"Yeah, yeah, we'll be okay," Brad said with a dismissive wave of his hand. He was trying to remember the current balance in his money market account. He would have to check on that tomorrow. "Plus, they're giving me a month's severance pay, so it'll turn out all right." He hoped he sounded more certain than he felt. "So anyway, did you guys see that game last night? What a bonehead, but lucky for us."

◆ ◆ ◆

"So, Brad, any luck on the job hunt?" Michael asked. Three weeks had passed since Brad's layoff and the guys had been carefully avoiding the subject, but Michael didn't want Brad to interpret their silence as a lack of interest or concern.

"Not so far," Brad replied. "I've been working with a head-hunter who's really trying hard, but there just aren't many openings in my field. Too bad I wasn't born a few years earlier. Remember when the building market was the hottest thing going?"

"Yeah, well, those days will come around again," Todd said. "They always do."

"Well, in the meantime, being unemployed is no fun. And it's very expensive. Our mortgage payments are pretty stiff, because when we bought the house we assumed my salary would keep going up instead of disappearing. Plus, now we've got to have a COBRA plan so we can keep our insurance and that thing is outrageously expensive. I never appreciated how much it helped having the firm kick in the lion's share of our health insurance premiums."

"Can't you get on Emily's insurance?" Todd asked.

"Are you kidding? She designs gift baskets. There are only three people who work in that little store and they don't offer insurance at all. My plan is all we've got, and the premiums will increase even more when the baby comes. Right now, we're on a member-plus-spouse plan, but the family plan costs more. And it's too late to change our minds about the baby now, right?"

"True," Todd said with a smile. "Nick, you're not saying much tonight. What's going on in that thick head of yours?"

"I was just thinking about my sister Carol. She's kind of going through the same thing, but her situation is a little bit different," Nick said.

"What's her story?" Brad asked. He appreciated his friends' concern and support, but was glad to have the group's attention turned to something else.

"She's the family genius. She got a degree in finance from NYU and started her own business right out of college, which takes guts. I'm not sure what she does. Some kind of investment advisor, I think. Anyway, she's a real whiz at the stock market, so she started right away buying this and that. She talks about it when she visits or we talk on the phone, but you guys know me. That stuff goes right over my head, so I just nod along. She and her kids are here visiting our parents, and at dinner last night she said her business went under."

"Really? Why?" Michael asked.

"Kind of like Brad, I think. Just economic downturns. It wasn't making money anymore so she closed down. But the good thing is that she's got all these investments, so she's okay. The family millionaire, in fact."

"Lucky her," Brad said wistfully. If the balance in his money market account kept going down, soon he wouldn't even be the family thousandaire.

◆ ◆ ◆

Several weeks later, Brad sat at the desk in his family room, paying that month's bills and watching his bank balance sink lower and lower. His wife came into the room and sank heavily onto the sofa.

"Hey, how are you feeling?" Brad asked.

"Pretty good. Just tired of getting kicked in the stomach by someone I haven't even met yet," Emily said.

"I know, but it won't be long now. You can hang in there a little longer."

"Yeah, I'm fine. What are you doing?".

"Paying the bills."

"Ouch. How are things looking?"

Brad hesitated before answering. He didn't want her to worry but, at the same time, he needed to be honest with her.

"Not that good, to tell you the truth."

"Oh! How bad is it?" Emily sat up a little straighter and looked at her husband with concern.

"At this point, we have enough cash for another month . . . maybe six weeks of expenses. And that's assuming we don't run into an emergency like a big car repair bill or storm damage to the roof or . . . aliens move into the basement," Brad said, trying to keep his voice somewhat light.

"Not to worry, our homeowner's insurance has an alien evacuation rider. I made sure of that," Emily said. She tried to match Brad's tone even though mounting panic was rising in her chest.

"See, that's what I like about you. Always thinking ahead."

"Seriously, Brad, what are we going to do?"

"Actually, I talked to my brother today. He said a job just opened up and it's mine if I want it."

Emily couldn't believe what she was hearing.

"He owns a furniture store. You're an architect."

"Not at the moment," Brad said, more than a little bitterness creeping into his voice.

"I know but . . . seriously? You're going to sell furniture?"

"Emily, what choice do I have?" Brad stood up and began pacing the floor. "Nobody is hiring architects now, at least not here in Chicago. I guess I could look out of town, but do we really want to move? This is home for both of us, and especially now with the baby coming, we want to be near our families. I grew up with my grandparents nearby and I want our kids to have that too."

"I do too. I'm not saying we should move. I'm just saying . . . I don't know what I'm saying. It's just that . . . your brother's store is in Gurnee. That's an hour's drive, and even more when the traffic is bad. And you'll have to work evenings and weekends . . . and I don't even want to think about the pay cut."

"I know, I've thought about all of that, but again, what are our choices? I've got to have a job and right now, that's the only thing available, unless you want me to flip burgers."

"I know, I get it. I guess we're lucky to have that option. At least it's an income."

Brad sighed heavily and sat down next to his wife.

"Yeah, that's how we have to look at it. It's not like it's forever. Carl knows I'll be leaving as soon as I can snag a position in my field, and he's fine with that. And I *will* get another job. Things will turn around, and in the meantime we don't have to think about drastic steps like selling the house." *Yet*, he thought.

"Well, tomorrow I'll tell Denise that I'll be coming back to work after my maternity leave," Emily said quietly.

Brad waited for a moment before speaking. He knew how excited she'd been about staying home with the baby, but now that wasn't an option. He was glad she'd brought it up so he didn't have to.

"I really didn't want it to come to that, Emily, but I think you have to. At least until things turn around."

"It's all right. Lots of moms work, and Denise has said she'd be flexible about my hours. She'll be happy that I'm staying, and my mother will be *really* happy that she'll get to watch the baby."

"Yeah, we might never get him back."

"I just don't understand how everything fell apart so fast," Emily said. "Two or three months ago, we were doing great. You had a great job . . . we had money in the bank. It's not like we're big spenders. It happened so fast."

"I guess the problem was that we didn't have *enough* money in the bank. We'd saved up a big chunk, but we took most of it out to make the down payment on the house. Then we had extra expenses with moving and buying furniture, and we never got a chance to build our savings back up again. I knew the firm was struggling financially, but it never occurred to me that I'd lose my job, or that I'd have so much trouble finding another one. I had three offers when I graduated, remember?"

"That seems like a long time ago now."

"Yes, it does."

"When do you start the new job?"

"I'm going in at one o'clock Thursday afternoon to fill out my paperwork and start learning the ropes. I guess Carl will give me my schedule then."

Emily turned and gave Brad a thoughtful look.

"I'd definitely buy a new dining room set from you."

"No, you wouldn't," Brad said with a laugh. "We can't afford it."

◆ ◆ ◆

It was Tuesday night again and the guys were gathered at McGuire's as usual.

"How's the furniture business?" Michael asked.

"It's okay," Brad replied. "I made a couple of good sales over the weekend, so the commission will be nice. The other sales people are good to work with and they've been helpful, even though I guess we're competitors."

"Is it weird to work for your brother?" asked Todd.

"A little, I guess, but he's been really cool about it. He knows I'm grateful for the job, but he hasn't rubbed it in or anything like that. Of course, I get the worst shifts since I'm the new guy, but that doesn't bother me. It just feels good to be working again. If I'd been home much longer, I might have started watching *The Young and the Restless*."

"Don't worry, we would have arranged an intervention before we let you sink that low," Michael said.

They all laughed, including Brad. It felt good to be out with his friends and know that he had a job to go to the following day. Not a great job, but a job.

"By the way, I won't be here next week," Nick said.

"Big date?" asked Todd.

"No, I've got to go to New York to help my sister move."

"Is she parting with some of her millions to buy a bigger place?" Michael asked. "Seems like she'd just hire movers instead of roping in her little brother."

"No, just the opposite," Nick said. "She's moving back to Chicago and staying with our parents."

"Why would she do that? She's loaded. You said so yourself."

"Not anymore, it seems. I told you her business went under."

"Yeah, but you said she had all those investments. It sounded like she didn't need to work at all."

"Things kind of took a turn. For some reason, she was really high on this company called Oxford Corporation. I think it's some kind of pharmaceutical company. Apparently a couple of her friends work there and told her about this great new drug that was coming onto the market, and they said all the stockholders were going to make a ton of money. Carol looked into it and it sounded great. The FDA was just about to approve the drug, so she decided to get in. She sold almost all her other investments and put everything into this Oxford thing. Everything was fine for a while. The drug hit the market like gangbusters and her money was earning almost 30 percent, which was a lot more than she'd been getting before."

"So what happened?" Brad asked.

"It all fell apart. Turned out the drug wasn't as great as everybody thought. They took it off the market, but by then 20 or 30 people had died and a bunch more had filed a class action lawsuit."

"Wait a minute, are you talking about Florigard?" Michael asked.

"I don't know, I think that's it."

"Don't you watch the news? That story has been all over the place."

"I get my news from ESPN, man. You know that."

"Well, you should broaden your horizons," Michael said. "Apparently the company had put almost all its resources into that one drug because it was so promising. Now they're being forced to fold up under the weight of all the lawsuits, not to mention the horrible publicity. Did Carol sell her stock?"

"No, and I guess now it's too late. She says it's worthless now."

"But you said she was a millionaire," Brad said.

"Hey, I design web sites for a living," Nick said with a shrug. "Michael's the numbers guy around here."

"I guess she was just a millionaire on paper," Michael said. "All her money was tied up in investments, and even worse, all with one company. A stock certificate isn't worth anything until you sell it, no matter how big the numbers are on your statements. Carol didn't sell her shares in time, the company went under, and now she's stuck with a bunch of worthless paper. She didn't have any cash in the bank?" He was careful not to sound critical, since his own financial situation was still precarious. He was in no position to take a superior attitude.

"I guess she has some, but not enough. Living in New York is even more expensive than here, and she's divorced with two kids. Mom and Dad suggested that she and the kids move back home for a while until she gets back on her feet, and she's taking them up on it. So that's the long story about why I won't be here next week. She's selling a lot of her furniture and stuff, then I'm flying to New York and helping her drive back here with the rest."

"How's Carol taking all of this?" Michael asked.

"Okay, I guess. I think she feels kind of stupid, but mostly she feels bad for the kids. She thought she was giving them a secure future, but instead, her mistake is forcing them to leave their home and their friends. They're pretty upset about it, but she doesn't feel like she's got a lot of choice. You know my sister though. She'll land on her feet."

Michael and Brad nodded in agreement and the group fell silent. Finally Brad spoke up.

"Remember when you were little and you had a piggy bank on your dresser, and every time your parents gave you money, you'd drop it in there?"

"Mine was a bear, but I do remember," Nick said.

"Every night my dad would take the change out of his pocket and divide it between Carl and me, and I'd run to my room to put my share into my bank. After I dropped it in, I'd pick up the bank and feel the weight. I'd move it up and down, and the way it got heavier and heavier every week felt great. That was real money, you know?"

"Real money," Michael echoed thoughtfully.

Brad continued reminiscing, his lips curling in a slight smile as he looked into the half-empty beer glass he held between his hands.

"When our piggy banks would get full, we'd empty them and Mom would take us to the bank branch in our neighborhood. The teller would run our money through the coin counter and come back with however many bills our change had translated into. My parents made us put half of it into our savings accounts, but we got to keep the other half. It was a great feeling to walk into the toy store with a few crisp new bills in my pocket, fresh from the bank teller's drawer."

"Real money," Nick said with a small laugh.

"Real money," Brad said, his thoughts slowly returning to the present. "You know, when I get back into architecture, and Emily and I are back on our feet again, I'm going to sock so much money into savings that the bank will have to add on an expansion just to hold all of it. I'll even design it for them."

"Great idea!" Michael said. "Then you can put your earnings from that design job back into your account."

"Exactly, my friend."

Nick took another sip of beer. "I think I've got about $500 in the bank," he said. "Maybe less. I've just never thought much about saving, but lately I've started to realize maybe I should start. I mean, if you and Carol can get blindsided, you know it's just a matter of time for a screw-up like me."

"Well, I wouldn't call you a screw-up," Brad said with a laugh. "But you really should start saving for a rainy day, as my dad would say. Emily and I thought we were fine, but when I lost my job, it was astonishing how fast we went through our savings. I was thinking we might have to sell the house until I got this job, and we're still struggling since I'm making less."

"How about you, Michael?" Nick asked. "Have you got a great big nest egg in case that company of yours finds out how little you really know and kicks you to the curb?"

Michael signaled the waitress for another round. This was his opening. These were his friends. His oldest and best friends, and they'd been open about their financial struggles. He should do the same. He took a deep breath.

"You'd better believe it. So . . . what about Saturday? Are we going to go together, or just meet at Wrigley?"

The Secret Explained: A Few Points to Remember

- In both your business and personal affairs, don't underestimate the importance of having enough cash on hand to meet any emergency.
- It's possible for a business to be profitable technically, but still go under because of inadequate cash flow.
- Don't make the mistake of tying up all your assets in investments that you'd need to liquidate if you needed quick cash.
- Having access to cash also enables you to take advantage of personal and business opportunities when they arise.

What's Your Skinny Cow?

- Are you so focused on making money that you allow all your assets to be tied up in long-term investments, leaving you completely exposed if the need for cash arises?
- Are you unrealistic about the possibility of job loss or long-term disability and the effect the loss of income would have on your life?

The 7 S.E.C.R.E.T.S

SECRET 4

Rate of Return

Do you understand the difference between an average rate of return on an investment and the real rate of return? Money masters do. So do financial advisors. Unfortunately, many of them don't want to share that knowledge with us, their customers.

Calculating and expressing the rate of return on investments is an area in which Wall Street wizards routinely perform the same kind of sleight of hand tricks we might expect to see at a top-notch magic show.

When David Copperfield mesmerizes us by making an object disappear and reappear right before our eyes, some degree of diversion is usually involved. When your financial advisor enthusiastically recommends a particular mutual fund and announces that it has a 20 percent average rate of return, he's also using a diversionary tactic.

In both cases, the trick usually works. Why? Because we want to believe. Deep inside, most of us really don't want to know how skilled magicians accomplish their tricks because it's more fun to believe it's really magic.

The same isn't true of your broker's sleight of hand. Learning how the trick is done can prevent you from making uninformed and potentially expensive investment decisions.

Rate of return—also referred to as return on investment, or ROI—is expressed as a percentage of the total amount invested, and it is usually calculated annually. There are several ways to calculate it, but the most typical way is by measuring the average annual rate of return. However, it's important to understand that average returns don't always translate into dollar returns. Let's look at an example.

Suppose you invest $100,000 in a great-sounding mutual fund recommended by your financial advisor. During the first year, there's a downturn in the market and your investment drops by 50 percent. You can't sell now because you'd lose $50,000, so you swallow hard and stick with it. Sure enough, the following year the market rebounds and your investment goes up 100 percent.

"Great news!" says your broker. "We had a positive 50 percent return over two years. That's a 25 percent average gain per year. See, I told you it was a good investment."

It certainly sounds good, but look at the bottom line on your earnings statement. Is your account now worth $125,000? Of course not.

During that first year, when your investment went down 50 percent, you were left with $50,000. The following year, it went up 100 percent. You doubled your money, but since you'd previously lost half of it, your account is now back to $100,000, the exact amount of your original investment. That's a *real* rate of return of zero.

But practically speaking, you have actually lost money. During that two-year period, you've had to pay management fees, and chances are good that inflation has also gone up, so your initial investment is now worth less than the day you handed that $100,000 over to your broker.

And while you're scratching your head, trying to make sense of it all, your broker is using that 25 percent average rate of return to convince another client to invest in the same mutual fund.

That, ladies and gentlemen, is the Wall Street version of sleight of hand.

Is this legal? You bet it is. The problem is that few people understand enough about investing to know how the rate of return really works, and few financial advisors take the time to explain it to their clients. Why? Because it's in the broker's best interest to keep us in the dark. That way, they can continue convincing us to make more investments on which they earn all those fees we talked about earlier.

At least with David Copperfield, you get dinner and a show.

Maximizing Your Returns

Now that you understand a bit more about different methods for calculating and expressing rates of return—and what they really mean to you as an investor—let's talk about a few ways of making sure you get the highest return possible.

Understand the Relationship between Risk and Reward

There's no way around it—in the investment world, risk and reward go hand in hand. The asset classes with greater potential for high returns, and those with the best track record for long-term performance, are also those with the greatest fluctuations in value.

Historically, the stock market has always had ups and downs, sometimes dramatic ones. But history has also proven that despite its volatility, it always comes back and, over time, it has always outperformed any other asset class.

The key to taking advantage of the market's potential for providing a high rate of return is patience. Investors who make money in the market are usually those who are able to resist the urge to buy and sell on a whim. They have a long-term investment plan and they stick with it.

Clearly, then, the market isn't the place to invest money you'll need to access soon, let's say in the next couple of years when your oldest child is ready for college. You might be thrilled and encouraged to see your investment climb steadily in the first six months, for example, but you might also watch it drop precipitously in the months before you'd planned on cashing it in to pay the tuition bill.

The stock market is volatile. Always has been. Always will be. But if you have time on your side, you are likely to get a higher rate of return from stocks than you would from other vehicles.

Know Your Risk Tolerance

Money masters know that all investors are not created equal. Some are gamblers, some are terrified of losing a single dime, and some are in between. Knowing which category you fall into can determine how well you sleep at night while your money is working for you.

Gamblers have the highest tolerance for risk. They're likely to keep the bulk of their investment dollars in the stock market because they're not afraid of the inevitable ups and downs. They're aggressive with their investment strategies and shy away from bonds and other vehicles that offer a lower level of risk in exchange for a lower rate of return.

True gamblers have nerves of steel when it comes to their money. They don't panic when their investments take a heart-stopping dive, because they know the decline in value is likely to be short term. They have faith that their stocks will rebound, and usually they are right because the overall market has a long history of recuperating from periods of loss.

At the other end of the spectrum is the investor with a serious case of risk aversion. In extreme cases, these people stay away from investments entirely, preferring to keep their money in the safety of a savings or money market account, or certificates of deposit.

They might dip a toe into government bonds, and if they have a 401(k) or other retirement account, they make sure it's invested in the vehicles with the lowest possible risk. If they do decide to venture into the stock market, they are likely to choose stocks they perceive to have the lowest risk, and they panic and sell at the first sign of a reduction in value. Ironically, they're more apt to lose money by selling rather than by riding out the vagaries of the market, which only proves to them once again that they are right to avoid risk at all costs.

The third group, which probably includes the majority of casual investors, takes a moderate stance. They balance their portfolios almost equally between the higher-risk stock market and the lower-risk vehicles like bonds and U.S. Treasury inflation-protected securities.

Knowing which group you fall into and planning your investments accordingly will help you get the highest possible rate of return without causing migraines and ulcers.

Diversify, Diversify, Diversify

The best way to lower your risk while maximizing your return is to spread your holdings over a broad spectrum of asset classes. This is the same principle as not putting all your eggs in one basket, as we discussed in Chapter 2.

The reasoning behind diversification is that while all markets are cyclical, they don't all move in the same direction at the same time. When real estate takes a dip, the auto industry might be on an upswing. When the U.S. stock market is sinking, the Asian market might be experiencing a major surge.

Spreading your investments through a number of different asset classes has been proven to deliver higher returns over the long haul and eliminates the extreme risk of putting all your investment dollars into a single company that could go belly up. Remember the lesson learned from those unfortunate Enron employees who had a little too much faith in their own company, as well as investors who thought the dotcom boom would last forever.

You don't have to be a stock market junkie to put together a diversified portfolio. Mutual funds, index funds, and exchange-traded funds provide instant diversification without forcing you to choose individual companies or industries into which you'll invest.

Different funds have different goals, so it should be easy to find one that matches your risk tolerance and overall investment goals. But before investing, be sure to look for funds that have the lowest possible fees and expenses. Otherwise you stand to give up a good chunk of your profits.

Take Advantage of Dollar Cost Averaging

Dollar cost averaging refers to the practice of investing a specific amount of money on a regular basis, as opposed to trying to time your purchases for periods during which the market is down and prices are lower.

By investing a little each month, sometimes you'll get lucky and buy low. Other times, you'll catch the market on an upswing and pay more for the same stocks than you would have paid a few weeks earlier. The idea is that, over time, it averages out.

There's another advantage to dollar cost averaging. If you invest the same amount each month, when you buy low, you will automatically get more shares for your money. On the other hand, when the market goes up, you will be paying more for whatever you're adding to your portfolio that month, but you'll also be potentially earning more. The additional shares you were able to purchase when prices were lower will enable you to reap the returns of the market's rise.

Don't Chase Hot Stocks

Money masters know better than to get caught up in the game of "what's hot right now." They realize that once a particular stock heats up enough to start drawing attention, the price has already been driven up. Sure, it could go higher, but it's doubtful that it will continue to rise enough to give you the rate of return you'd have received if you'd bought it before it got hot. You will benefit more by sticking with your long-term investment strategy.

• • •

A week after their initial meeting, Melissa found herself seated in Dan Burton's office again, this time by herself. "You don't need me," Ben Guilford had said. "I think you made a good choice, so you and Dan can take it from here. Let me know if you run into any problems."

Dan came into the office and handed her a cup of coffee.

"Cream, no sugar, right?" he said.

Melissa took a sip. "It's perfect. Thanks."

"You're welcome. Just let me know when you're ready for a refill. Are you all right? You seem a little nervous today. Are you having second thoughts about working together?"

"Oh no! Not at all," Melissa said quickly. "I have complete confidence in you. I guess the problem is that I don't have confidence in myself. Not in this area anyway."

"What do you mean?" Dan asked.

"I tried to do some reading over the past few days so I'd understand a little more about all of this, but it's intimidating. I'm one of those right-brain people. Trying to understand investing takes me back to my high school days."

Dan smiled. "Math wasn't your best subject, huh?"

"That's an understatement," Melissa said with a laugh. "Algebra was my worst nightmare, except that I was wide awake and it went on for months. I got really good grades in most of my subjects. I was the artsy type. I got tons of awards in art, played oboe in the orchestra, and acted in plays, but I also did well in the academic subjects. English, social studies, psychology—they all made sense to me. I even did all right in science, but math lost me pretty early in the game. By the time I got to algebra, it was a lost cause and the teacher didn't make it any better."

"How so?"

"Mr. Sutherland was really intimidating, or at least I thought so. He'd ask these rapid-fire questions and I was never quick enough, so I lived in a perpetual state of embarrassment and humiliation. I dreaded having to go to the board because I hated having everyone watch me struggle with the problems. I was kind of shy to begin with, so that didn't help. He had a handful of favorites—the kids who were the math whizzes and destined to become engineers or something. Maybe it was just my imagination, but it seemed like he enjoyed singling me out and making me uncomfortable. One day—the worst day—he had been quizzing me for what seemed like an hour about some formula I couldn't wrap my brain around. Finally he let out a long sigh and said, "Melissa, I give up. This stuff is so easy, but you just don't get it. I used to think that you weren't studying, but I've changed my mind. I think you're just one of those girls who can't do math.""

"He really said that to you? In front of the whole class?" Dan said. "That's unbelievable."

"Oh, he said it. The good news was that he quit picking on me after that. He pretty much just ignored me from then on, like I didn't even exist, which was fine with me. I squeaked along for the rest of the semester and felt lucky to come out with a D. But looking back, I can see how that helped shape my feeling that I can't understand numbers, and that part of the reason is that I'm female. Maybe that's why I chose a boyfriend who's an accountant. If we end up getting married, someone will be there to help the kids with their math homework!"

"A forward thinker. I like that," Dan said with a laugh. "But seriously, Melissa, you need to retool your thinking a little bit. It's completely true that all of us have different strengths and talents. If I had to make a living as a designer, I'd starve in a week, but you work for one of the top agencies in Chicago."

"Yes, but you don't have to design your company's ads. I know that I'm hiring you to do the heavy lifting in terms of my investments, but I feel like I need to understand the whole concept more, and instead I feel like I'm back in Mr. Sutherland's class and he's pointing out that I'm just a dumb girl."

"Well, first of all, let me dispel a myth for you. Would it surprise you to learn that women often make the most successful investors?"

"Yes, I guess it would. Is that true?"

"It is. Not only have I seen it in my own practice, but I've also read studies that bear it out. Women are more likely to learn from their mistakes, so they usually don't make the same mistake twice. A lot of men treat their investments almost like a hobby. They like to be buying and selling all the time, so if they're working with a broker who works on commission, they rack up so many fees that they barely make a profit. Men are also more likely to be gamblers."

"What does that have to do with investing?" Melissa asked, picturing a casino filled with blackjack tables, roulette wheels, and slot machines.

"For example, they tend to hold onto a stock too long. When it goes up, they refuse to sell because they think it will keep going higher. Women are more likely to sell when the stock is high and take the profit, rather than taking a chance that it will drop again."

"That's interesting. I didn't know that, but maybe they are the girls from my class who really understood all those algebraic formulas," Melissa said.

"Maybe, maybe not," Dan replied with a smile. "I don't know where you got the idea that you have to be a math genius to invest money."

Melissa hesitated before speaking. This was going to prove once and for all that she was an idiot.

"Well, like rate of return. A few days ago, some people in my office were arguing about who was getting the best rate of return on their investments. One guy said he was getting 18 percent on some stock and somebody said that was impossible. Then they kept going back and forth about how it was calculated and whether it was averaged over some number of years, and my eyes just glazed over."

"I'll admit that rate of return is a confusing area, mostly because a lot of brokers talk in terms of an investment's average rate of return, and that can be spread over a number of years. I'm sure that's what caused the confusion between your friends."

"It *is* confusing," Melissa said. "Shouldn't there just be one system so everybody is on the same page all the time?"

"You'd think so, but unfortunately, that's not the case. Let me tell you a story that I heard at a conference a year or two ago. I thought it was a good illustration of how this business works sometimes."

"Okay."

"It seems that there was a shipwreck and a few of the survivors managed to swim to a small island. There didn't seem to be anyone around, but while they were exploring the area to see what resources they might find, one of them spotted a can of beans. Obviously this was a happy discovery because they were getting pretty hungry at that point, but their excitement faded when they realized they had no way to open the can. They sat for a few minutes, looking at the can and thinking. The first one to speak up was a physicist.

"'I've got an idea,' he said. 'We'll climb up that hill over there and roll the can down. When it crashes against the pile of rocks at the bottom, it will break open and we'll eat.'

"One of the other guys was a chemist. He said, 'No, that won't work. When the can breaks open, all the beans will spill and they'll be ruined. I've got a better idea. My lighter still works, so we'll gather up some dry grass and wood, and we'll start a fire. When we heat the can over the fire, eventually the pressure will build and the can will open.'

"'That's not going to work either,' the physicist said. 'The can won't open. It will explode and the beans will fly everywhere. That's no better than my idea.'

"'I guess you're right,' the chemist said. Then he turned to the third man, who was an economist. 'Do you have any ideas?'

"'Actually, I do,' the economist said. 'Let's assume we have a can opener.'

"That's the situation we're talking about, Melissa," Dan continued. "We have a tendency to assume too much. In this case, most investors assume that the way their rates of return are calculated and expressed are equal, but they're not."

"I see . . . " Melissa said hesitantly, but it was obvious that she was still confused.

"Let me give you an example," Dan said, reaching for a pad of paper and a pen. "Let's say we took half of your inheritance and invested it in a mutual fund."

"All right," Melissa agreed, thinking that she wasn't quite sure what a mutual fund was, but she didn't want to ask another dumb question.

"Rates of return are usually calculated annually, so a year from now, I send you a statement showing how your investment has performed. Unfortunately, it's been a tough year for the stock market, and I have to report that your investment has lost 60 percent of its value."

"Can that happen?" Melissa asked, a note of panic entering her voice.

"Anything can happen, but this is just an example. I'm not going to let that happen to you," Dan said.

"Now I only have $4,000, right?"

"Exactly. But you committed to staying in this investment over the long haul, so you resist the urge to panic and get out, and it's a good thing, because the market does a complete turnaround and at the end of the year, you've made a 100 percent return."

"I've doubled my money! That would be good."

"It would, but how much money do you have now?"

Melissa looked at the figures Dan had scribbled onto the pad.

"Oh. I see. I was down to $4,000, so if I double it, I have $8,000."

"Exactly. See, you're not so bad at math after all. Here's the trick though. When we calculate the rate of return on that investment over a two-year period, the average will be 20 percent."

"But I have less money than I started with. How can I have a 20 percent rate of return?"

"Because it's been averaged over a two-year period. That's why you have to look carefully when someone touts an average rate of return. You need to dig a little deeper and figure out what the *actual* rate of return has been on each year you've held the investment. It's possible to have an impressive sounding average rate of return, but if one of the years was extremely good and the other extremely bad, you could have lost money."

"That's misleading."

"It certainly can be."

"Thanks for explaining it to me," Melissa said. "I see what you're saying, but in a way, that just makes me even more nervous about investing. I don't really understand money. My parents never talked about it when we were growing up, except that my dad would sometimes tell us how my grandparents had lost a lot of money in the stock market. I guess I'm afraid of it. Sometimes there are stories on the news about people who make a fortune in the market, but it seems to me like there are more stories about people who've lost their money. I don't know, maybe those are just the ones that stick with me, but now I actually know someone who had a bad experience."

"What happened?" Dan asked.

"It was the sister of my boyfriend's friend, Nick. She made some kind of bad investment and ended up losing everything she had. Now she and her two kids are back living with her parents."

"That's a shame. I always hate to hear stories like that, but I can assure you, they are not as common as you might think. I don't know anything about that particular case, obviously, but I'd be willing to bet that she made some bad decisions."

"See, that's another thing," Melissa said. "All of this seems to require a lot of decision making, and I'm not sure I'm all that good at it, especially when it comes to this kind of thing. I feel like I make a million decisions at work every day and I don't know if I want to come home at night and be faced with decisions about which stock to buy."

"I know exactly what you mean," Dan said. "We're all on decision overload. Yesterday my wife called and asked me to pick up a few things at the grocery on my way home from work.

She wanted toothpaste, bread, and milk. Sounded simple enough to me, so I didn't even write it down. Normally I just stop at a convenience store, but on the way home I got a craving for lamb chops, so I went to the supermarket instead. There I was in our neighborhood Food 4 Less, staring at the milk display in utter amazement. Let me tell you, they don't have nearly that much variety at the 7-Eleven. Whole milk, 2 percent, 1 percent, skim, soy, rice, lactose free . . . finally I closed my eyes and visualized our refrigerator and realized that my wife bought the one with the light blue cap, so problem solved."

"That was smart of you," Melissa said.

"Well, that wasn't the end of it. The bread aisle was no better. There were probably six different kinds of whole wheat alone. Finally I spotted the brand we usually get, but that didn't help much. They had five-grain, seven-grain, twelve-grain, fifteen-grain . . . I didn't know that many grains even existed, much less baked into one loaf of bread. I must have had a deer-in-the-headlights look because a woman standing next to me started to laugh and I realized she was laughing at me."

"What did you do?" Melissa was laughing too, picturing Dan looking at a long row of bread in total bewilderment.

"She said, 'Did you get sent to the store?' and I said, 'Yeah.' Then she pulled a loaf off the shelf and said, 'Try this one. It's healthy, but kids usually like it.' I tossed it into my cart, thanked her, and got away from that aisle as quickly as I could."

"I don't blame you! So you still had to get . . . what was the other thing? Toothpaste?"

"Yep, and I'm sure you can guess how that went."

"I know! Why do we need so many kinds? Whitening with mouthwash, whitening without mouthwash . . . it's crazy. Did you find the right one?"

"I picked one that looked like it had everything and hoped for the best. All I kept thinking was that if I chose wrong, I'd be right back here looking at 428 kinds of toothpaste again."

"Well, at least your wife only wanted three things. It could have been worse."

"Actually, it was. As I was heading for the checkout lanes, I passed the cookie aisle, and I thought I deserved a treat after all that. I've loved Oreos since I was a kid, so I thought I'd grab a package real fast. When did Oreos get so complicated?"

Melissa was laughing hard now. He was right. Everything involved another decision.

Dan was enjoying her amusement, so he ramped up the drama a bit, gesturing wildly.

"I was happy when they came out with the double-stuffed ones, but now they have golden ones. Did you know that? That's not an Oreo. Oreos are chocolate. And cake ones! What's that about?"

"How about the ones covered in chocolate? Did you see those? And there are seasonal ones . . . purple stuffing in the spring, red at Christmas."

"You've got to be kidding."

"I'm afraid not."

"Well anyway, that was the long, drawn-out way of saying that I agree with you. We have far too many decisions to make about even the simplest things like toothpaste and cookies, so it's no wonder decisions about how to invest money seem so overwhelming."

"That's exactly what I'm worried about," Melissa said, getting serious again. "The first financial advisor I talked to just wanted me to give him a check and let him make the decisions. After I talked to Mr. Guilford, I realized that it was probably a bad idea, but now I'm thinking maybe it would be easiest thing to do—just give you the money and let you decide on the best way to invest it for me."

"I won't let you do that, Melissa. I'm flattered that you would trust me that much, but it's not how I work. I'm not going to ask you to look at a long list of individual stocks and pick some, but I want you to be actively involved in the process. I can provide guidance, but we'll make the decisions together, okay?"

"That sounds good. Where do we start?"

"I've been looking over my notes from our first meeting, and one thing I realized is that I'm not completely clear on where you see yourself in the future."

"I'm not sure what you mean."

"You're young and your life might change a lot in the next few years. You could get married, have children, buy a house, move to another city or even another country, start your own business . . . there are a lot of possibilities for someone your age, and they might affect how we invest your money."

"I'm not sure, to tell you the truth. Michael—that's my boyfriend, Mr. Guilford's son—Michael and I have been together for a while, but we haven't talked seriously about marriage. I'd like to get married and have kids, but I'm not in a hurry, if that's what you mean." She was glad Ben wasn't here for this conversation. Talking about the future of her relationship with Michael in front of the man who could potentially become her father-in-law would be acutely uncomfortable.

"That's fine, Melissa. I'm not suggesting that you need to have your future mapped out before we can make investment decisions for you. I'm just saying that there might be considerations to take into account."

"Like what?"

"Well, for example, if we're going to put your money into stocks, I'd recommend that you plan to leave those investments untouched for about ten years."

"Why is that?"

"It gives you a chance to ride out the ups and downs of the market. Sometimes your stocks will be down and sometimes they'll be up. That's just the nature of the beast, but you'll get your best results by letting your money work for you over a longer period. Suppose we invested all of your money in stocks today—don't worry, we're not going to do that; I'm just giving you an example. We put all $20,000 into the stock market and three years from now, you decide you want to pull it out to make a down payment on a house. Call me a pessimist, but I'm a big believer in Murphy's Law. You know? The theory that anything that *can* go wrong *will* go wrong?"

"Yeah, I believe in that too," Melissa said with a smile.

"Well, with Murphy's law being what it is, I can almost guarantee that the day you come to me and ask me to cash out your investments, the market will be on a downward slide and you'll lose money. So what I'm asking is whether you foresee a circumstance in which you'll want access to your money in the next ten years."

"I can't say for sure," Melissa replied. "I don't have any plans to buy a house, but I guess that could change, so no, I wouldn't want all of it to be tied up for the next ten years, and I wouldn't want to be in a position of losing money if I had to take it out."

"That makes sense." Dan looked down and shuffled through his notes. "You told me that you have about $2,500 in savings, right?"

"Yes, I put some money from every paycheck into savings. My parents taught me that."

"It's a smart move. Do you know how much interest you're getting on it?"

"I'm not sure but in my last statement, I'd earned about $20 in interest."

"That's less than 1 percent. Better than no interest at all, but we can do better."

"Great."

"The first thing I'm going to recommend is that you move your current savings into a money market account, and that we put $3,000 of your inheritance in there as well."

Here we go again, Melissa thought. Such a dummy.

"I hate to sound like a moron again, but I'm not sure what that is. I've heard of them, but that's it."

"A money market account essentially works the same way as a savings account, but there are a few differences. You can write checks against the funds, and often even use a debit card, but your money earns a higher interest rate than it would in a standard savings account. There are some restrictions, so we'll have to shop around to get the best deal for you, but I'll help you do that. Some of them have minimum deposit amounts, but with more than $5,000 you'll qualify for a good one. We'll avoid any with minimum balance requirements, just in case you need to get your hands on the money in an emergency, and we'll look for one that doesn't have a lot of expenses and fees. It's hard to believe, but sometimes those can be higher than your interest rate. Sometimes there are fees if you go over a set number of checks per month, so if you write a lot of checks you might want to keep your current checking account too. Otherwise you can just use the money market account if you want."

"I pay most of my bills online, so usually I only write a check for my rent," Melissa said.

"Then a money market fund is a good option for you. I'll find one that suits you best, including the highest interest rate available, and we'll get that set up for you. I think it will make you more comfortable to have a bit more of a cushion, and you can keep contributing something from each paycheck until you get enough for several months of expenses, just in case the worst happens."

"That sounds great. What about the rest of the money?"

"I think mutual funds are the right way to go for you," Dan said. He hurried into an explanation, not wanting Melissa to have to ask. Clearly her lack of knowledge was a source of embarrassment. "Mutual funds essentially are a pool of money that's been contributed by a lot of individual investors. The fund has a manager, or sometimes a group of managers, who invest the money for you."

"How do they invest it?"

"That's a good question. It depends on the goal of the fund. Some are set up for long-term growth, some are designed to provide a steady income for investors, and some are a combination. It's a good way to make sure your investments are diversified, because the fund manager buys a lot of different stocks and, as an investor in the fund, you own a little bit of each of those companies. You don't have to make decisions about which stocks to buy because the manager does all that and keeps you and the other investors informed regularly. It's also a good system because you don't have to pay commissions every time the manager buys or sells an individual stock. There's a management fee, but we can find one that's reasonable."

"That sounds really good," Melissa said. The explanation made sense and she was relieved that Dan wasn't going to call her every day with recommendations for buying and selling shares of Widgets, Inc.

"There's another consideration," Dan went on. "What I just described is a managed fund, because the manager is in charge of making decisions about what stocks to buy and sell, and when to do it. There is another type called an index fund. Those buy the entire group of stocks and bonds from a particular group like the Standard & Poor's index of 500 stocks, or all the stocks in the NASDAQ stock market. It's the same principle as a mutual fund, but with an index fund you own a little bit of every company on that particular index."

"That sounds even better," Melissa said. "I'd be more diversified, right? And I'd be less dependent on the skills of the fund manager. It would be automatic." Had she just used the word "diversified?" Was this stuff starting to make sense?

"I think an index fund would be a good option for you, especially if it makes you feel more comfortable. That's a big part of investing. You have to go with what you feel comfortable with. We mentioned gamblers earlier. Some people are okay with the roller coaster ride. They get a thrill out of taking chances, but I don't sense that you're one of those people."

"Not where my money is concerned."

"That's fair. You have to learn to trust your instincts, and my sense is that yours are good."

"Thanks. So how do we pick a fund? Or will it be more than one?"

"A lot of it depends on your age and how much of a risk taker you are. We've established that you're not much of a gambler, but you're also starting young, so you can afford a little more risk. I'll never push you outside your comfort zone, but you've got a lot of years left to work and invest, so now isn't the time to be ultraconservative. I'm going to recommend a couple of options that will give you maximum growth potential without keeping you awake at night worrying about your money."

"That sounds like a great approach."

"Good. The other thing you need to remember is that we can always make changes as we go along. I'm not saying that I'm going to keep you in the same investments until you retire. As your life changes, we'll adjust."

When Melissa left the office, she looked at her watch. She had half an hour until her next meeting, so she decided to enjoy the beautiful day and walk back to her office rather than grabbing a taxi. She had expected to feel exhausted from all the talk about topics that were foreign to her, but instead she felt exhilarated. She'd handed a cashier's check for $20,000 to Dan Burton, and instead of being petrified, she felt great about it. The pieces were starting to fall into place. The process was slow, but she was starting to catch on, and most important, she was learning to trust her own instincts.

As she walked along busy Michigan Avenue, she flipped open her cell phone and called Michael's number. He answered on the third ring.

"Hey, what's up with you today? I tried to call you earlier but I got your voice mail."

"I've been busy," Melissa said. "Congratulate me. I'm an investor."

The Secret Explained: A Few Points to Remember

- The *average* rate of return on an investment over a particular period of time is not the same thing as the *actual* rate of return.
- The investment classes with the highest rate of return are also those that experience the most volatility.
- There are ways to balance the risk/reward equation, including diversification, dollar cost averaging, and being patient with the inherent volatility of the markets.

What's Your Skinny Cow?

- Are you losing both money and sleep by buying and selling stocks every time there's a change in the market?
- Do you allow a financial advisor to talk you into investment strategies that go directly against the level of risk you're comfortable with?
- Are you easily snowed by investment jargon, leading to the possibility that you don't know what actual rate of return you're getting on your investments?
- Are you afraid to ask questions if you don't understand a term or concept?

The 7 S.E.C.R.E.T.S

Economy

Imagine that your favorite recreational activity is playing golf. You play 36 holes every weekend, so you're pretty darn good. You consistently beat everyone you know, and people often tell you that you should consider playing professionally.

One sunny Saturday afternoon, you're at your favorite course with a buddy. You're feeling confident because you know this course like the back of your hand. In fact, you have a number of birdies and even a couple of holes in one to your credit. Just as you're stepping up to the first tee, your friend says, "How about if we change it up a little?" He reaches into his back pocket, pulls out a blindfold, places it over your eyes, and ties it behind your head. "Okay, tee off whenever you're ready," he says.

It's a totally different game now, isn't it? You'll be lucky to keep the ball on the fairway, much less get it onto the green.

In the world of money and wealth, the economy is like that fairway. It's the big picture. If you can see it spread out in front of you and you know where the sand traps and water hazards are, you've got a much better chance of getting on the green than if you're swinging away in the dark.

Let's pause for a short history lesson. Back in 1944, while World War II was still raging, delegates from all of the Allied nations met in Bretton Woods, New Hampshire, to establish a set of institutions and rules to regulate the international monetary system. Among other things, the resulting Bretton Woods Agreements required each country to base the exchange rate of its currency on a gold standard.

Now fast forward to 1971. With its gold supply depleting rapidly and unable to meet demands, the United States removed its currency from the gold standard, making the U.S. dollar the sole backing of its currencies and, in effect, making it the international currency. Today international transactions always take place in U.S. dollars.

What does this mean for the economy? Since our currency is no longer required to be backed by an asset like gold or silver, if we want more money in the system, we can simply print more. The more money we have floating around out there, the less each dollar is worth. Inflation, remember?

How the Banks Do It

Do you know who makes the greatest amount of money in our economy? Banks. And they do it by understanding and using two basic economic principles—the velocity of money and positive arbitrage.

If you have a $5 bill in your wallet and we asked you how much it was worth, most likely you would think the obvious response would be $5, but that is not exactly true. A $5 bill is just a piece of paper. It only takes on worth when it's exchanged for something.

The velocity of money refers to the speed at which money changes hands. If it's not moving, it's worthless. If it's moving slowly, it's worth less than before.

Let's look at an example. Suppose that, back in 2005, you went into a store to buy a widget that cost $20. You pulled a $20 bill out of your wallet, but before you reached the checkout counter, you had second thoughts. You returned the widget to the shelf, stuffed the money into the pocket of your jacket, and went home.

Five years later, when the first autumn chill hits the air, you get that jacket out of the closet. You reach into the pocket and are surprised to find the $20 bill. Finding money unexpectedly is always fun, so you decide to treat yourself.

You return to the same store to buy the widget that you passed up back in 2005, but guess what? Now the price is $22.20. If you'd exchanged that piece of paper for the widget five years ago, it would have been worth $20. Now, because it has been parked in your jacket pocket for five years, it's only worth $17.80.

In a moment, we'll talk about how banks use the velocity of money to make a profit, but first let's understand the second principle: positive arbitrage. Here's how it works. Suppose you go into a bank and deposit $5,000 into a money market account that pays 1 percent interest. The bank can afford to pay that interest because, while your money is in the account, the bank borrows it and uses it to make money for itself. We typically think of banks as the lenders and us as the borrowers, but in reality, banks make their profits by wearing both hats simultaneously.

As you are walking out of the bank, deposit slip in hand, your neighbor, John, is coming in to sign the papers for his car loan. Let's make it easy and say that he's borrowing $5,000. Rather than the 1 percent that you're receiving on your money market account, the bank will charge John 6 percent interest. The difference—in this case 5 percent—is arbitrage, and it's how the bank makes money. As John pays off his loan, the bank will turn that money around just as quickly as it did your $5,000.

The point is that the bank doesn't let your money sit around getting dusty. It keeps it moving constantly, and it does so in ways that continue to turn a profit. While your money is parked in that account, you're earning interest, so you could consider the situation a win-win, but who's winning more?

From the time we're children receiving our first piggy bank, we are taught the value of saving. Usually it's ingrained in us that we should put our savings somewhere that is considered safe— a bank account, a 401(k), a certificate of deposit—and leave it there until we need it. Undoubtedly, as we discussed in Chapter 4, it is important to have a nest egg so that we are prepared for emergencies, but to build real wealth we need to learn how to get the bulk of our money moving as quickly as possible, before inflation has a chance to catch up to it.

Because, let's face it: If you're not taking advantage of the wealth you're creating, someone else is.

Beyond Our Borders

Money masters know that it's not just about the U.S. economy anymore. What happens in this country has an effect on money and investments around the world, and vice versa.

One often-overlooked way to diversify an investment portfolio is to look for opportunities outside the United States, because although the United States still boasts the world's largest economy, it doesn't always outperform those of other nations. While investing overseas can be lucrative, there are also some caveats to consider.

Each year, *Forbes* magazine publishes its Global 2000, a listing of the largest, most powerful, publicly traded companies in the world. The United States still leads the pack by a good margin, but its dominance—and in fact, the dominance of the world's developed nations as a whole—is steadily receding.

In the list released in April 2010, 11 of the top 20 companies were headquartered somewhere other than the United States. Of the top 50, a whopping 31 were foreign-owned.

Let's take a closer look at those 50 most powerful companies in the world. Six are Chinese. In fact, China has three businesses in the top 20 and 114 scattered among the 2000. It's impossible to ignore the rapidly increasing influence of China on the global economy.

Seven European nations are represented—France, the United Kingdom, Germany, Italy, Spain, Switzerland, and the Netherlands. Russia and Japan are also represented in the top 50, along with Australia, South Korea, Canada, and Brazil.

The point is that the world keeps getting smaller and an ever-increasing number of countries are getting a piece of the global economic pie. It only makes sense to consider that trend when we are making decisions about how to invest our money.

At the time of writing, the United States, while certainly not out of the woods yet, is slowly showing signs of emerging from the economic debacle that started in 2008, while at the same time several European countries are experiencing severe crises of their own. As the world's developed nations continue to struggle, investors are increasingly turning to so-called "emerging" countries for investment opportunities.

There are good reasons for that trend. When the recent economic meltdown hit, those emerging market countries didn't take nearly as big a hit as our own economy did. Those markets are also growing considerably faster than ours as their consumer spending goes up.

Let's take a look at a couple of specific examples and talk about what money masters see when they consider foreign investments.

China

China's economy is growing at a rate that is nothing short of stunning. Operating on a growth model that focuses on saving rather than spending—just the opposite of the U.S. model of "spend it all today and let someone else worry about it later"—China's foreign exchange reserves now top $24 trillion and are expected to continue to grow by nearly $500 million a year. Two-thirds of those reserves are held in U.S. dollars.

It's not just the country's cash reserves that are growing. China's gross domestic product is increasing at a rate of about 10 percent a year, while our GDP is growing at only about 3 percent. As their country continues to develop on many levels, the Chinese are investing heavily in technology as well as raw materials such as oil and minerals.

It remains to be seen how China will use its economic power, but many experts believe that, consciously or not, the country is in the process of reshaping the global economy in a way that will serve its own interests, perhaps at the expense of others.

So is it a good idea to invest directly in Chinese companies? Maybe, maybe not.

China has long had the reputation of being a land of mystery. In novels and movies, that can be a very romantic and enticing notion. Not so much when your money is at stake.

A great deal about China, including its government, social policies, and publicly traded businesses, remains shrouded in mystery. It's very difficult to get any information at all about individual Chinese stocks, and it's even harder to determine the accuracy of any bits of information you're able to find, so hand-picking stocks is probably not your best bet.

However, mutual funds and exchange-traded funds are much safer, and more of them are becoming available as investors' interest in China heats up. In the past couple of years, gains recorded by mutual funds that invest in China and other developing Asian markets have had about triple the returns of the S&P 500.

If you do decide to stick a toe into the Chinese economy, make sure it's only a toe. Money masters watch emerging markets with great interest, but they know better than to put too much money there. They also realize that emerging markets, by their very definition, experience a lot of ups and downs, so they take a long view of those investments, being patient enough to ride out the downswings and wait for the upswings.

Latin America

Another emerging market that gets a lot of attention these days is Latin America. Better fiscal policies, along with unprecedented political and social change, have led to a perception that many Latin American markets are more stable than in previous years, so more investors are eyeing opportunities there.

Lending credence to that theory is the fact that government bonds in Mexico and Chile have now been upgraded to investment grade for the first time. Additionally, in a two-year period Brazil's stock market went up more than 250 percent, leaving many investors salivating to get in on the action. In fact, Brazil attracted $37 billion in direct foreign investment in 2007 alone, prompted in part by its now-stable government.

What do Latin American countries have going for them? In many cases, commodities. Mining opportunities—silver, iron, copper, even emeralds—abound in many areas including Brazil, Colombia, and Peru. Mexico and Venezuela are among the world's top oil producers.

Many of the same problems inherent in direct investment in China also exist in Latin America. There is little information available on individual stocks, and political corruption continues to be rampant in many countries.

Assessing Your Risks

Money masters never go into a business opportunity without first taking a hard look at the potential risks, and overseas investments carry some unique ones that should not be overlooked.

In addition to market risks that are inherent in any part of the world, foreign investments might carry political risk as well. The Middle East is the most obvious example, but many countries in other parts of the world have governments that are relatively unstable. In addition, some risk is incurred when power changes hands in the United States or another developed nation. A new U.S. presidential administration brings with it the potential for a shake-up in the country's relationships with other nations around the world, particularly those with which the United States has been on shaky ground in the past.

International investing also carries currency risk. The value of any country's currency with regard to another's goes up and down routinely. Is your investment protected if the pendulum swings the wrong way?

Many investors got caught in that very situation a few years ago when Colombia became one of the hottest real estate markets in the world. Many people took advantage of opportunities to buy property there, and they were elated when property values went up 40 percent in one year. Unfortunately, that same year the value of the U.S. dollar went down about 40 percent against the Colombian peso, yielding an actual rate of return of approximately zero.

You will also want to make sure you are on solid legal ground before getting involved in foreign investments. Just as the United States has laws and policies to regulate how other countries and their citizens purchase assets here, other nations have enacted similar measures.

• • •

It was Saturday night, and Michael and Melissa were driving to his parents' house for dinner.

"I'm excited about meeting your brother," Melissa confessed.

"Why? He's just a guy," replied Michael.

"I know, but I don't know much about him. You and I have been dating for two years and you hardly ever talk about him. Do you not get along?"

"Oh no, we get along fine. It's just that he's a lot older than I am, so we've never been very close. He was 15 when I was born, so I was just three when he left for college. He came home for vacations, but after he graduated he got a job in San Diego and he's been there ever since. When I was growing up, we went to visit him a few times and he comes back here every couple of years, but we've never had much in common because of the age difference. He's a great guy. I guess he just seems more like a cousin than a brother because of the age difference. Plus, if you want to know the truth, I was always a little jealous of him when I was growing up. He was kind of a golden boy—stellar athlete, straight-A student—so I always felt like people were comparing me to him."

"Oh, come on. Your parents are so proud of you."

"I know they are. It's just that there would always be stories about Matt making the winning touchdown in a football game, or getting a bunch of scholarship offers when he finished high school. When people came over to the house, they would always ask, 'How's Matt?' 'What's Matt up to?' 'Do you think Matt will ever move back to Chicago?'"

"I'm sure they didn't mean anything by it. They didn't have to ask about you because you were still here. They knew what you were doing."

"Yeah, I guess you're right. Anyway, you'll like him. Everybody likes Matt."

When they arrived at the house, the first few minutes were filled with the usual greetings and introductions. The Guilfords were clearly thrilled to have their oldest child home for a few days, and the warmth he felt toward his family was evident. As they gathered around the dinner table, Melissa took advantage of the opportunity to observe Matt. He was tall and good looking, with thick, dark hair and the chiseled features that so many men in his profession seemed to possess.

"Michael tells me you're a TV anchorman," Melissa began.

"Yeah, I'm kind of an anomaly in my business," Matt said. "I started at the network affiliate in San Diego as a reporter right out of college and eventually, when the anchor slot opened up, I got promoted."

"That doesn't happen much, does it?" Melissa asked. "It seems like people move around a lot in the television industry."

"They do, but I got lucky and found a home right away. I like San Diego and apparently the people there like me, so I've been able to stick around. That's not to say I won't get fired tomorrow, but if I do, I've got plenty of money saved, so I would be okay until I found something else."

"How much?" Michael asked. The words slipped out before he thought about it and he instantly regretted saying them. He had a feeling he was about to feel vastly inferior to his successful older brother once again.

"Michael!" his mother exclaimed in horror. "That's none of our business."

"It's all right, Mom. I don't mind," Matt said. "More than $240,000."

Inferior indeed, Michael thought. He should have gone to Matt for a loan instead of his father. He imagined that his dad was thinking the same thing, and drawing a pretty unflattering comparison between his two sons in terms of their ability to manage money.

"That's great, Matt," Ben said. "What are you invested in?" He loved to talk about investments and hadn't realized his oldest child was interested in them too.

"Bank of America," Matt replied.

Ben's fork stopped midway to his mouth.

"All of it? Invested in a bank stock? In this economic climate? You've got to be kidding."

"No, not in Bank of America stock," Matt said. "It's actually *in* Bank of America. You know, in a savings account."

This time Ben put his fork down completely. He hardly knew what to say. Everyone at the table was stunned. Michael took a deep breath, waiting for his father to heap praise upon Matt for being such a good steward of his money. What happened next was a complete surprise.

"Have you lost your mind?" Ben asked. "You've got almost a quarter of a million dollars in a savings account? *A savings account?*"

"You always told us to save, Dad," Matt said. What was the problem here? "The bank's assets are insured. The money is safe. It's not going anywhere."

"Well, you've got that right," Ben said, still incredulous over what he'd just heard. "It's not doing you much good either."

"What are you talking about? I get 1.5 percent interest. That's almost $4,000 a year for doing nothing."

"And that's enough for you?"

"It took me a long time to save that money, Dad. I don't want to risk losing it in the stock market."

"You could invest in government bonds," Melissa said. "The rates are higher but they're not as risky as stocks, especially if you choose carefully. There are some available in foreign governments that are paying 5 or 6 percent."

Everyone turned to look at her.

"When did you become an authority on investing?" Michael asked.

"I'm not," Melissa said. She hadn't even realized she'd spoken until everyone's eyes were on her. "My financial advisor has been helping me and I've been doing some reading on my own. But don't listen to me. I'm incredibly new at this. Pretend I didn't say anything at all." And please stop looking at me, she thought.

"No, Melissa, you're right. Bonds are a much better alternative than a savings account. It's important to have enough cash available to cover a few months of expenses, but beyond that, it's just foolish to have all your assets sitting in the bank. There are a lot of ways to get your money working for you. It's just a matter of finding the right ones for you."

"That's what Dan says," Melissa said. "He's my financial advisor. I can't believe I have a financial advisor. I have a financial advisor." Was she really talking again? Shut up, Melissa, she thought.

But she didn't.

"He explained to me that money isn't any good unless you're spending it on something. Like a $20 bill in your pocket is just paper, but if you spend it on something like a DVD, then the cost of the DVD becomes its worth. I didn't explain that very well."

"No," Ben said. "You're exactly right. Having money in the bank works on the same principle. When it's in a bank account, the bank is paying you a low interest rate, but they're lending the money to someone else at a much higher rate. That's how they make their money. In your case, Matt, Bank of America is making a very healthy profit—maybe $20,000 or $30,000 a year—on your $240,000 and you're making less than $4,000 on it. So who is that money really working for?"

"The bank," Matt said thoughtfully.

"Again, I'm not saying you shouldn't have a nest egg in cash. I've always told you that and I still believe it," Ben said.

Michael took a bite of mashed potatoes and thought about Brad, as well as Nick's sister, Carol. He wondered if either of them would ever again think their nest egg was big enough, even if they had $1 million in cold hard cash buried in the back yard.

He turned his attention back to the conversation. His father was still speaking.

"I'm just saying that there are a lot of ways you can get your money to work for you instead of the bank, even if you don't think the stock market is the right investment route for you."

"Dan says it's like trying to lose weight," Melissa said. "I'm sorry, that sounds stupid. I'll shut up. Sorry." Way to make a good impression, Melissa, she thought. When we leave, they'll have a good laugh about Michael's chatty girlfriend who talks about things she knows nothing about.

"No, go ahead," Michael's mother said encouragingly. "What do you mean?"

"Well, he says that there are lots of different ways to lose weight, and not all of them are right for everybody. You can go into a bookstore and find hundreds of books with different ideas and diet plans, but none of them work if you don't actually put them into practice. Low carbs might be right for one person, but that might be a nightmare for someone else. He says the key is to find the diet—I mean, investment program—that's right for you personally, and then go into it with a positive attitude. Dan says it's hard to make money if you're always afraid of losing."

Michael looked at Melissa with interest. How many times was she going to quote this broker, or whatever he was? Surely she didn't have a crush on him. It would be humiliating to have his girlfriend dump him for some middle-aged guy who swept her off her feet talking about return on investment and shareholders' equity. Maybe he should meet this Dan guy.

"That's a good point," Ben said. "Have I told you the story about the two groups of soldiers who went on a hike?"

Only about six times, Matt thought, glancing across the table at his brother. Michael responded with a slight roll of his eyes, but Melissa was leaning forward with interest, so neither of them spoke up.

"Somebody in the Army brass decided to do an experiment to test the effect their attitudes had on soldiers. They started with 2,000 soldiers and divided them into two equal groups. These weren't new recruits who were still in the first weeks of boot camp. They were tough, battle-hardened guys who'd seen combat and survived. The commanding officer told the first group that they were about to embark on the most difficult march they'd ever had to make. He told them they'd be going over a long distance of rough, mountainous terrain, and that the weather would be hot and muggy. To make it even harder, the weight of their backpacks had been doubled over what they would ordinarily have carried.

"When the hike was over, three-quarters of the soldiers said it was the worst, most grueling hike they'd ever endured. Several of them had gotten sick during the march, and some weren't even able to finish and had to be driven back to their base camp in jeeps.

"The second group was told a completely different story. The commanding officer told them that because they'd been working so hard in their current training exercise, they were going to be rewarded with one of the easiest hikes they'd ever taken. He said the terrain wouldn't be challenging, the weather conditions were going to be ideal, and they'd be carrying packs that were only half as heavy as they were used to.

"At the end of the day, all 1,000 soldiers completed the hike easily. No one got sick, no one had to be driven back to camp, and 89 percent agreed that it was one of the easiest hikes they'd ever taken. Do you know what the catch was?"

"They'd gone on the same hike?" Melissa guessed.

"Exactly! All 2,000 soldiers had walked 14 miles over the same terrain in identical weather conditions and carrying the same weight in their packs. The difference was in their attitudes. The ones who were expecting the worst got it, and those who had better expectations had a better outcome." Ben sat back in his chair with an air of satisfaction. He loved a good, inspiring story.

"I see your point," Matt said. "I guess I should get some of that money moving instead of sitting there making profits for the bank. I still don't think the stock market is the right place for me, but a while back I thought about buying some rental property."

"That might be just the right thing for you," Ben said. "Property values in California have really taken a hit, so a guy like you with cash to spend could buy property for pennies on the dollar."

"Yeah, that's what I was thinking. I actually was working with a guy for a while. He showed me a bunch of properties, but I just couldn't seem to pull the trigger."

"Why not?"

"I don't know. I guess I was just scared of losing my money. This guy probably showed me two dozen properties, but when it came time to sign a contract, I chickened out every time. Finally he quit returning my calls, and I can't say I blame him. I was just wasting his time."

"Well, you're never going to get your money working for you if you just leave it in the vault," Ben said. "Why don't you do some investigating? Maybe you could take a course or find a partner who has some experience in real estate investing to work with you. You've lived there long enough to know the area pretty well, so you should be a good judge of which areas are likely to be good investments. You know prices are going to go up again, so you're lucky you have the opportunity to get into the market when they're at rock bottom. Think of it this way— you'll be stimulating the economy while you're making more money for yourself. And I know you well enough to know that you're not going to scam anybody. You'll be giving someone a good home at an affordable price, and you'll still be making a nice profit. But you're going to have to pull the trigger soon. Imagine how you'll feel if you wait another year and property prices have gone up by then? Regret isn't a very pleasant companion."

"I think you're right," Matt said. "All of a sudden, I'm starting to feel enthusiastic about it again, and I know a couple of people who might make good partners, if they're willing. And I do like the idea of helping to stimulate the economy, even if it's in a small way. It gets depressing to keep reporting those terrible numbers night after night on the news."

Ben raised his wine glass in a toast. "Good for you," he said. "Bank of America's loss is California's gain."

The Secret Explained: A Few Points to Remember

- Money isn't worth anything until it is exchanged for something.
- If you don't keep your money moving at a fairly rapid rate, inflation will cause it to lose value.
- The world's developing nations are becoming an increasingly important contributor to the world economy. The potential for investing there can be a good way to diversify a portfolio and should not be ignored, but proceed with caution.

What's Your Skinny Cow?

- Do you have all your money tied up in a low-earning savings account because you're afraid of the risks inherent in investing it?
- Do you lose money to inflation because you don't keep it moving?

The 7 S.E.C.R.E.T.S

Tax Efficiency

Federal tax

State tax

Sales tax

Local tax

Gift tax

Transfer tax

Deed tax

Probate tax

Business tax

Property tax

Stamp tax

Income tax

Payroll tax

Self-employment tax

Welcome to the great state of Taxes! Everything really is bigger here, and destined to get bigger still.

As these words are being written, the U.S. national debt stands at more than $12 trillion, and it increases by more than $4 billion every day. To get out of this sorry situation, the government has two choices. It could dramatically increase inflation, driving down the worth of the dollar to almost nothing, or it could raise taxes exponentially. Which scenario do you think is most likely?

Most Americans already think they are paying too much in taxes, so it's only natural that when we hear about ways to cut our tax bill, we listen eagerly. For young men and women who are just out of college and starting their first jobs, that orientation program they attend on the first day of work typically includes a lengthy sales pitch about the company's 401(k) program. Your money can grow tax free! That's right! You won't pay a dime in taxes until you retire and begin drawing it out *30 years from now*! Wow, sign me up!

Back up and take a closer look.

Obviously we need something other than Social Security payments in order to have a comfortable retirement. When the Social Security program was created, it was designed to carry each recipient through only a year and a half. Life spans were shorter then, so most people died within a relatively short time after they retired. The ratio of active workers to retirees was significantly larger, too—about 30 workers for each retiree, as opposed to about 6 to 1 now—so many, many more people were paying into the system than were taking out of it.

Today, everything has reversed. People draw Social Security for an average of 15 years after they retire, and the amount of money being paid into the system has shrunk dramatically. No wonder the system is going broke.

Clearly it's essential for people to find other sources of retirement income, and a 401(k) sounds like a good option. After all, we are a nation of procrastinators, so we might as well put off paying taxes on that money for as long as possible.

We will tell you why that is not such a good idea, but to fully understand, you need to know why the 401(k) was created in the first place.

The stage was set by the Tax Reform Act of 1978, through which Congress planned to offer taxpayers breaks on deferred income. Benefits consultant Ted Benna is widely credited with having a light bulb moment in which he realized that the new tax code could be used to create a tax-friendly vehicle that would enable employees to save for retirement. Soon, the rules under which the plans would operate were established and the 401(k) was off and running.

Why do you suppose the federal government wanted to encourage deferring taxes on our income in the first place? It wasn't purely benevolence on the part of Uncle Sam, that's for sure. The powers that be had begun to look into their crystal ball and they saw a huge problem looming a few years down the road—baby boomers.

When servicemen returned home from World War II, they did what all returning servicemen do, and as a result, between 1946 and 1964, the population of the United States increased by a whopping 30 percent. As boomers have aged, their sheer numbers have affected everything, from which cars sell the most, to what we watch on television, and what kinds of products pharmaceutical companies develop. It was no accident that Viagra hit the market just as a large segment of the population began to need its benefits.

It's only natural that, by the late 1970s, the government had begun to consider how this large number of people would affect the country's resources as they moved through life. They realized that, as the boomers retired, not only would the strain on the Social Security system become untenable, but also the tax base would be adversely affected as millions of people presumably would begin paying far less in taxes as their incomes dropped after retirement. The solution, obviously, was to find a way to tax them later. Hello, 401(k).

The system works out great for the government, and for those who make a living from the money we park in the same spot for 30 years. Unfortunately, it doesn't work quite as well for a proud owner of the 401(k), who begins drawing out the money after 30 years of inflation and tax hikes have dramatically decreased its value.

Here's an example. Bob the Boomer began working full time in 1980 and eagerly opened a 401(k) immediately. He faithfully contributed to it over the years and now is ready to retire and begin enjoying the fruits of his labor.

On the day he packs up his desk and gets his gold watch, his account balance stands at $400,000. Not bad! The only problem is that every dollar that Bob withdraws from his account is taxed at today's rates, not those that were in effect at the time he contributed that dollar. Add the 163 percent inflation rate between the day Bob started work and the day he retired, and it's easy to see that his retirement nest egg isn't worth what it could be.

But Bob is lucky. He has received a large inheritance and doesn't need to use his 401(k) to pay his living expenses and support his lifestyle. He thinks he'll just leave the money in his account and let it keep working for him.

Sorry, Bob. The government has taken care of that issue with something called required minimum distributions. When Bob reaches age 70½, he will be forced to start withdrawing the money from his 401(k) whether he wants to or not. After all, if it continues to sit in his account, all cozy and tax deferred, Uncle Sam won't get his share.

That's the situation we're faced with today. In the next few years, 30 percent of our country's population will begin taking money out of their 401(k) accounts. As they liquidate those investments, the stock market inevitably will go down, just as it went up in the late 1990s.

The dotcom boom got the credit for that market surge, but there was a larger factor that received less attention. It was the boomers again, hitting their peak earning years and shoveling as much money as possible into their 401(k) accounts as they began to think about retirement. Thirty percent of the population was buying stocks at the same time. No wonder prices rose.

Still think a tax-deferred savings plan is in your best interests? Let's look at it another way. Imagine that you're a corn farmer. It costs $1 to buy a bag of seed that eventually will yield a profit of $1,000. You have to pay 25 percent in taxes, but you can decide whether to pay it when you bought the seed or when you sold the crop. The choice is simple, right? Deferring the tax until you sell the corn would cost $250. Paying it on the seed would cost 25 cents.

Many argue that since people are likely to be in a lower tax bracket when they retire, it makes sense to pay tax on the harvest rather than the seed. Obviously, this is a matter that should very seriously be discussed with your personal financial advisor. Let us share two specific thoughts. First, the notion of retiring at age 70 is no longer a reality for many, if not most, people. So the idea that we will be in a lower tax bracket is a thought from the past, and not keeping up with today's reality. Second, are taxes likely to go up or down? While we don't have a crystal ball, it is a pretty safe bet that taxes will go up. If that's so, then by paying taxes on the harvest rather than the seed, we will be paying a higher amount on a higher percentage. That's not a good plan!

When we put money into a deferred tax 401(k), we're choosing to pay taxes on the harvest, not on the seed.

Finding Tax Efficient Investments

Money masters know that the real return on an investment isn't what you initially earn on it. It's the amount that you get to keep, and the more Uncle Sam gets, the less is left for you.

The good news is that it's possible to limit the damage by finding investments that have fewer tax consequences than similar instruments, and taking the time to look for them can make a big difference in how well your investment dollars work for you in the long run.

Stocks

If you're a hands-on investor who enjoys picking individual stocks, be aware that the tax consequences can vary based on the type of stocks you choose and how you handle your portfolio.

You'll get to keep more of your earnings by selecting stocks that don't pay a dividend. Why? Because dividends represent capital gains. Each time you receive one, you'll be taxed on it.

Also, don't be too quick to buy and sell. We've already discussed several benefits of investing for the long haul to avoid the volatility of the market, but there are also tax advantages to holding your stocks for a longer period of time. If you sell stock and make a profit within a year of purchasing those shares, you'll be taxed at the short-term capital gains rate, which is higher than the long-term rate for shares held more than a year.

Mutual Funds

For managers of traditional mutual funds, taxes aren't necessarily a concern because the funds themselves aren't taxed on profits from the sale of the securities they hold or on income from dividends. For investors, who are taxed on both capital gains and dividends, they're a huge concern.

Fortunately, there are an increasing number of tax efficient mutual funds available. In fact, many of them are easy to spot because their names include terms such as "tax efficient" or "tax managed." Don't just take that at face value. Information regarding the fund's historic tax costs should be available, so it's smart to look into it before making an investment decision.

Fund managers have several options for limiting tax liability for their shareholders. They can focus on buying tax-free or low-tax vehicles such as municipal bonds. They can also avoid turning over the fund's holdings too often, thus ensuring that investors' capital gains are taxed at the lower long-term rate. A third option is limiting the fund's investment in stocks that pay dividends, since investors will be taxed on each dividend they receive.

Indexed Life Insurance

We are both big fans of using certain types of life insurance policies as investment vehicles. Specifically, we use Indexed Life Insurance, or IUL. We must quickly add a caveat here: Handle With Care! When created properly, IULs can be an incredible wealth-building tool as part of your portfolio. The challenge is that the vast majority of life insurance agents have absolutely no idea how to create an IUL that will minimize fees, commissions, and the cost of insurance. When created properly, IULs are often the tool of the wealthy. Imagine having the ability to access the gains of the market without the downside risk of the market? A properly formulated IUL policy can do exactly that, and, with the right company and in the hands of experts, may add elements of safety, asset protection, cash flow and rate of return, with incredible tax-efficiency, that combine to add a very strong and positive element to your portfolio.

In Trusts We Trust

One of the benefits of accumulating wealth is the ability to pass it down to your heirs, but money masters look for ways to do it without saddling the beneficiaries with a major tax bill. Establishing a trust can be a good way to do that.

For example, a Grantor Retained Annuity Trust is potentially more tax efficient than simply letting your heirs inherit your money at the time of your death. These trusts enable you to make large financial gifts to family members without incurring the U.S. gift tax.

This is how it works. The grantor sets up an annuity trust, deposits money into it, and receives an annual payment from it for a fixed period of time. At the end of that period, or upon the death of the grantor, the trust's beneficiary receives the remainder of the money as a gift. The IRS has a complex formula for determining how the trust's remaining value is taxed, but in most circumstances it will be less than the standard gift tax that would otherwise apply.

One final caveat: While it's a good idea to look for tax efficient investment options, don't let that be the only determining factor when setting up an investment program. Tax efficient vehicles should still fit with the rest of your portfolio and investment strategies.

Small Business, Big Rewards

For many people, starting a business and being their own boss is an important part of the American dream, and the United States tax code supports that dream by providing tax breaks for those who take the plunge. If you operate your business from your home, the advantages are even bigger.

Let's take a look at a few ways that starting your own business can help lower your taxes.

- **Office space**. If you set aside a room in your house to serve exclusively as your office, you can deduct not only the costs incurred in buying furniture and equipment, but also a portion of other home-related expenses such as a percentage of your mortgage payments and property taxes. A percentage of your homeowner's insurance and utility bills might also be deductible.

- **Mileage.** Keep a small notebook in your car and record all business-related mileage, such as traveling to meet a client or trips to the office supply store to pick up items needed for your business. This mileage is deductible at a rate set by the IRS, and if you pass the grocery store on your way, it's okay to stop in and kill two birds with one tax-deductible stone.

- **Business expenses.** such as subscriptions to work-related magazines and membership in professional organizations can be deducted.

- **Travel.** In some circumstances, travel might be deductible. For example, if you attend a business conference in Tucson and take the family along for a vacation, you can deduct the cost of your hotel room and rental car, as well as your airfare (but not theirs!)

- **Electronics.** If your home telephone doubles as a business phone, it's not deductible, but you can deduct the cost of a land line, cell phone, or Internet access that's dedicated to your business.

- **Educational Expenses.** Educational expenses such as courses necessary to develop specific skills needed for your business, including online courses and educational software, are deductible.

- **Associated Costs.** Meals and entertainment for business purposes are deductible, but be careful. This is a benefit that is often abused so the IRS tends to look carefully at those deductions.

But before you race off to convert the spare bedroom into a photography studio, please consider this. Tax laws change from time to time, and knowing exactly what small business expenses you can and cannot deduct can be tricky. It's absolutely essential to keep careful records and consult a qualified tax professional to avoid getting into trouble. This is a case in which a little knowledge can be dangerous, and you don't want to end up paying IRS penalties that might be higher than the taxes you were trying to save.

• • •

"Michael, say hello to Rafe Garcia. He's starting today as a senior accountant. Rafe, this is Michael Guilford."

Michael looked up from his spreadsheet to greet the office manager and the new hire she was taking around the office. He could barely contain his surprise when he saw Rafe. This was the new guy? He had to be at least 60 years old.

"Good morning, Rafe. Very nice to meet you. Welcome," Michael said.

"Good to meet you, Michael," Rafe said. "I'm looking forward to working with you."

The pair moved on, with the office manager pointing out the kitchen as she escorted Rafe down the hall, and Michael wasted no time going to the office of his colleague, Elise. They had started working at the firm within a month of each other and had become good friends.

"What's the story on the new guy?" Michael asked as he went into Elise's office and closed the door behind him.

"Rafe? I have no idea. I was going to ask you the same thing. He seems a little . . . experienced for a new hire, right?"

"I'll say."

There was a tap on the door and Justin stuck his head in.

"Hey, did you meet the old guy?" he asked.

"Yeah, we were just talking about him. Who is he?" Elise asked.

"I don't know the whole story. All I heard is that he's an old friend of Mr. Bradford. He needed a job, we had an opening, and here he is."

"Why would a guy that age need a job?" Michael pondered. "Maybe he got convicted of embezzling and just got out of prison."

"Yeah, like Bradford would hire an embezzler," Justin scoffed.

"Maybe his wife left him and took him for everything he had," Elise offered.

"Maybe," Michael said.

"Here's our chance to find out," Elise said. "I just got an e-mail asking if I'd take him to lunch to welcome him to the firm. You guys are on the list too."

Seated around a table at a small Italian restaurant near their office building, the four placed their orders and waited for the server to leave.

"So Rafe," Michael began. "Are you getting acclimated all right?"

"Yes, doing fine," Rafe replied. "First days are always hard, trying to remember everyone's name and learning where the staples are kept. Your computer system is a little different than the one I was used to, but I'm a fast learner. I'm sure it'll be fine. I'm looking forward to getting down to business."

Elise looked at him carefully. Maybe it was her imagination, but his enthusiasm seemed a little forced.

"Where were you before this?" Justin asked.

"I was retired. I spent 30 years at FitzGerald, Chase, and Monohan, and I retired almost five years ago."

"Oh," Elise said. "And now you're . . . unretired? You missed the work that much?"

"No, unfortunately that's not the reason I came back, although there were days when I did miss it. I came back because I had to. It was either that or cut way back on our standard of living, and my wife and I had both worked too hard to do that."

I'll bet he lost all his money in some crazy Ponzi scheme, Justin thought. He seemed too smart for that, though.

"Surely a big firm like FitzGerald has a 401(k) plan," Michael said. Seeing the look Elise shot him, Michael quickly began to back-peddle. "I'm sorry, Rafe. That's none of my business."

"No, I don't mind. You kids might as well learn something from my experience. They do have a 401(k) plan. They started it about two years after I joined the firm, so I jumped in right away. We all did. It seemed like a no-brainer to let that money build up tax free until we retired. I just kept making my contributions and didn't give it much more thought than that. As the time to retire got closer, my wife and I bought a place in Florida so we could spend the winters there and come back here in the summer."

"Snowbirds," Elise said.

"Right," replied Rafe. "When I hit that 30-year mark, I put in for my retirement, and Lisa and I started taking it easy. We did a little traveling and started thinking about buying an RV so we could take off whenever we wanted to. That probably sounds silly to kids your age, but we thought we'd enjoy it. We figured we'd take a couple of our grandchildren with us sometimes and see the country together."

"No, I think it sounds great," Michael said. "Did you get it?"

"No, about the time we were getting serious about it, the stock market took a really bad turn. I hadn't really kept up with things over the years, making adjustments as I got closer to retirement, so most of my money was still in riskier stocks and the account balance went down so fast it made me dizzy."

"That's awful," Elise said. "I don't think much about my 401(k) being invested in the market because I've got a long way to go before retirement and I figure the ups and downs will balance out over time, but I guess maybe having your retirement dependent on the stock market might not be such a good idea."

"Take it from me, it's not," Rafe said with a hint of bitterness in his voice. "Early on, the company made a 401(k) sound like such a great thing that I never bothered to think it all the way through to the end. Now I wish I'd done that instead of just believing everything I was told. Lisa and I are both in excellent health and expect to live for a long time. My parents are both still living and they're in their 90s, so unless one of us gets hit by a bus, we're probably going to be around for a while, and when we started looking at the numbers, we realized the money wasn't going to last as long as we would. I've moved it into safer investments now, but the balance took a pretty big hit. The only good thing about having less income is that it put us into a lower tax bracket. Saving in a tax-deferred account is great while you're saving, but not so good when you start pulling it out and have to pay those taxes. Now I wish I'd paid taxes on the money when I first invested it. My first ten years with FitzGerald, I was in a pretty low bracket, so I'd have saved a bundle by getting taxed on that money up front."

"I hadn't thought about that, but I guess it makes sense," Justin said. "We're probably in the lowest bracket we'll ever be in right now, but we're waiting until we're in a higher bracket to pay the taxes on our retirement savings."

"That's right," Rafe said. "When I first started my 401(k) Lisa and I figured up how much we thought we'd have when we retired and it sounded like a fortune. Thirty years later, between inflation and taxes and market hits, it's not enough, so here I am, back in the saddle. I figure I'll work another six or seven years and hopefully by then I'll be ready to retire again. By then the grandkids will probably be too old to want to go traveling in an RV with a couple of old geezers, but Lisa and I will still enjoy it."

The Secret Explained: A Few Points to Remember

- Your 401(k) was created in part to solve the government's tax problems, not yours. Take a closer look before assuming that it's the tax-saving miracle you've been led to believe.
- Some investment vehicles are more tax efficient than others. Take time to look into how much an investment might cost in taxes and see if there are ways to minimize the damage.
- Consider the potential tax advantages of starting your own business, especially one that you can operate from your home.
- Consult a qualified tax professional before getting too creative with home-based business deductions. They're perfectly legal and encouraged, but you can expect them to be carefully scrutinized by the IRS, so be sure you know what you're doing and keep immaculate records.

What's Your Skinny Cow?

- Are you losing money by ignoring opportunities to reduce your taxes, or flirting with danger by deducting business expenses that you can't back up with receipts and other records?
- Are you being unrealistic about the tax advantages you'll receive from your 401(k) and the implications of having that money taxed when you withdraw it?

The 7 S.E.C.R.E.T.S

Sense

It's Saturday night and you, a young woman, are at your favorite bar with a couple of your girlfriends. While you're waiting for the bartender to come back with another glass of wine, a great-looking guy strikes up a conversation. He's witty. He's charming. He's *British*, for heaven's sake, complete with the irresistible accent. You work in the same industry. You vacation at the same place. He's perfect. Your friends are forgotten as you continue to fall under his magic spell. Your friends signal that they're ready to leave, so you start to say goodbye, certain that he's going to ask for your number. Instead, he leans toward you, looks into your eyes and says, "I really, really like you. I think we've really got something here. Let's get married."

Does that make sense?

Your 11-year-old son comes home from school with a large rip in the left knee of his jeans. You just bought those jeans last week and they weren't cheap. You are understandably upset because his school doesn't allow students to wear clothes with visible patches and it's clear that there is no other way to fix that gaping hole. You ask him what happened. "Mom, it wasn't my fault," he begins. "I got off the bus and started walking home when a car pulled up beside me and a guy got out. He was wearing a black suit and sunglasses and he had a machine gun. He tried to grab me and make me go with him, but I ran away. He chased me down the street and he fired the machine gun at me, but you know how quick I am, so I was able to dodge the bullets. I ran as fast as I could and finally I climbed over the Conrads' fence, but their dog was in the yard and he started chasing me too. He tried to bite me, but he just got my pants in his teeth and I yanked my leg away, and that's when my new jeans tore."

Does that make sense?

It's 2:30 A.M. and you can't sleep. You get up, put on a robe, grab the mint chocolate chip ice cream, and head for the den to watch a little TV. The screen comes to life with an infomercial. Your finger pauses on the remote, ready to do some channel surfing, when the guy on the screen captures your attention. He's tall, tan, and totally ripped. Broad shoulders, impressive pecs, six-pack abs. And he's standing next to a life-size cut-out of himself 142 pounds ago. He was huge! Kind of like you'll be if you keep eating ice cream in the middle of the night. Soft, doughy, big gut. How did he change so much? Ahhh, he's telling you . . . and selling you. Take one of these magic fat-burning pills before every meal and within eight weeks, you can look like this too!

Does that make sense?

Just as in every other area of your life, your financial life needs to make sense. The world is filled with well-meaning but gullible people who want everything to come easily, so they spend their lives looking for the quick fix—the big lottery win, the business deal that's just around the corner, the get-rich-quick program that's available for a limited time at the low, low price of $99.

A web site called The Consumerist, a subsidiary of *Consumer Reports,* recently reported that one in three lottery winners is in serious trouble or even bankrupt within five years of hitting it big. Some have gambled away millions, and some have been taken by con artists, scams, and their own friends and relatives. Some have simply spent it all.

All of them suffer from the same affliction—failing to give careful thought and consideration to managing their money, and failures to use old-fashioned common sense in making financial decisions. It's a malady that's all too common not only among lottery winners but among ordinary investors as well.

Trust Everyone, but Cut the Cards

Money masters realize that if something seems too good to be true, it probably is. They don't take the word of any money manager, no matter how successful, at face value. They ask questions—a lot of questions. Then they get a second opinion, and a third one.

We've seen countless people over the years who have watched their portfolios drop as much as 50 percent before they woke up and took action. When asked how it happened, many have been quick to protest that they *did* get a second opinion . . . but they got it from another financial advisor in the same firm.

What if you received a bad medical diagnosis and told your doctor that you wanted a second opinion, only to have him hold up a hand puppet and give you the same advice? That wouldn't make sense, would it? Neither does relying on a second financial opinion from someone who is unqualified to give it, or who might have a vested interest in seeing your money go into a particular investment vehicle or be handled by a particular firm.

Some years ago, a very wealthy man took his young son on a trip to a Third World country so he could see how people lived in extreme poverty. The man felt that his son had always lived a life of luxury and privilege, and he wasn't appropriately grateful for all that he had been given. They spent several days with a poor family who lived on a remote farm, living a life that could not have been more different from theirs.

Traveling home on their private jet, the father asked the boy what he had learned from the experience. "I learned that we only have one dog, but they have four," the boy replied. "We have a pool in the middle of our yard, but they have a stream that goes on forever. We have lanterns in our yard, but they have millions of stars. Our back yard reaches the fence, but theirs reaches the horizon. We have a private yard, but they have fields that go on and on. We buy our food, but they grow theirs. We have servants, but they serve others. We have walls that protect us, but they have friends and neighbors who protect them. Thanks for showing me how poor we really are."

It's all a matter of perspective, isn't it? It's critical to look at your investments from every vantage point, and to get opinions from people who will look at them from a fresh perspective. Bottom line: After completing your due diligence, if you don't understand a proposed course of action, or if it doesn't feel right deep in your gut, don't do it. Use your common sense.

Let Your Values System Be Your Guide

In October 1982, seven people in Chicago died of apparent cyanide poisoning. It didn't take long for investigators to link the deaths to each other and trace them to a common source—tainted capsules of Extra Strength Tylenol.

Clearly this was a massive public relations nightmare for Johnson & Johnson, Tylenol's parent company. Before the poisonings, Tylenol enjoyed a 37 percent share of the painkiller market in the United States. Immediately after the public learned that the product had been responsible for the deaths of several people, its market share dropped to just 7 percent.

As the investigation continued, it was revealed that the problem had not occurred during the manufacturing or packaging process. It wasn't the result of negligence on the part of Johnson & Johnson, or the act of a disgruntled employee with an ax to grind against the company.

The tampering had taken place after the products had reached retailers. Someone systematically removed bottles of Extra Strength Tylenol from Chicago drug stores, added to the capsules more than enough cyanide to kill a human, then returned the bottles to the shelves.

It was obvious that Johnson & Johnson was not responsible for the tragedy, but the company accepted responsibility anyway. A massive product recall, which was completely voluntary, pulled every bottle from the shelves—some 31 million bottles from across the country. The effort was staggering, as was the cost to Johnson & Johnson. The company is estimated to have taken a loss of about $100 million.

All advertising for Tylenol products was immediately replaced with statements explaining the recall and other steps that were being taken to prevent anything similar from happening in the future. When Tylenol returned to the market, the pain-killers were encased in triple-sealed tamper-resistant packaging, and additional advertising dollars were spent to promote the caplet version.

Here's the important part. When company officials were asked what led to their decision, they replied that it wasn't a difficult choice at all. It seems that in the 1940s, then-chairman Robert Wood Johnson had written his company's mission statement. In a credo that is still in effect today, the first two sentences read.

"We believe our first responsibility is to the doctors, nurses and patients, to mothers and fathers and all others who use our products and services. In meeting their needs, everything we do must be of high quality."

It was as simple as that. There was no decision to be made. There in black and white was a statement written some 40 years earlier that told Johnson & Johnson's top executives what they needed to do.

Nearly 30 years later, that story is still cited as a case study in exemplary crisis management. The public was both protected and reassured, the company continued to thrive, and the product bounced back.

Why did it happen that way? Because Johnson & Johnson's leaders looked at the situation and made a values-based decision.

They did what made sense.

Which Will You Choose, Discipline or Regret?

In investing, as in every other part of life, the key to success is pretty simple. It's a few simple disciplines repeated over time. In the moment, small actions don't appear to have much of an effect, but when compounded over a period of months or years, the impact can be enormous. The trick is not to get discouraged if you don't see immediate results.

Suppose you watched Uncle Joe eat a pound of crispy fried bacon and shortly thereafter die of a massive coronary. The cause and effect would seem pretty clear, and you probably would make an immediate decision to cut bacon out of your own diet. But that's not how it works. It took years of daily bacon consumption for Uncle Joe's arteries to slowly clog until they reached the point at which they could no longer function.

To use a more positive example, Serena Williams didn't become a tennis champion overnight. It took years of faithful practice to perfect her stroke into that of a champion. With each stroke of her racket, she got just a little better, and although the difference was imperceptible on a swing-by-swing basis, the cumulative effect over time was dramatic.

If success is defined as a few simple disciplines repeated over time, it follows that failure is a few simple disciplines neglected over time. If you don't exercise today, you won't see or feel a difference in your physical condition and appearance tomorrow, but if you don't exercise for two years, will you see a noticeable difference? Absolutely. If I leave the house tomorrow morning without telling my wife that I love her, it might not make a difference that day, but if I neglect that simple discipline for a year, the result could be devastating.

Boiled down to its essence, your future financial success is a choice between two things—discipline and regret. Understanding the seven secrets of the money masters, applied with common sense and discipline over time, can help you build a secure future for yourself and your family—possibly for generations to come—rather than a legacy of regret.

• • •

"I'm really excited about having everyone over tonight," Melissa said. "We haven't seen Nick since our wedding, and when we get together with Brad and Emily, it seems like there's always chaos with the kids around. It'll be nice to have just the adults tonight."

"I know," Michael said as he helped chop vegetables for a large salad. "It seems like time goes so fast these days. Soon we'll be dead."

"Well, I wouldn't put it that way!"

It had been more than five years since Michael's crushing trip to the ATM. He had worked hard to get his financial life on track and although there were some bumps in the road, he was proud of his progress.

Before he proposed to Melissa, he finally confessed his financial sins. Although he was out of debt and had money in the bank by that time, his credit rating had taken a hit, so he couldn't justify starting their life together with something like that between them. Of course, he edited out a few of the more humiliating details, like the trip to the grocery with the jar full of change. Full disclosure didn't have to include *everything*, did it? They opted for a small wedding rather than a full-on extravaganza, and they worked together to rebuild his credit rating. The effort paid off, because their mortgage application was approved immediately and they moved into their three-bedroom suburban ranch just five months before the birth of their son, Nathan, a year ago.

Brad and Emily were the first to arrive.

"It's about time Nick came back for a visit," Brad said. "When he took that job in LA, I figured he'd be back within a year. He's a Midwestern boy, but I guess he's gone California on us."

"I don't think he's ever coming back at this point," Melissa said. "I ran into his sister at the grocery a couple of weeks ago and apparently there's a young lady on the scene now. She said it sounded serious."

"How is Carol?" Emily asked. "It's been ages since I've seen her."

"She's doing well. Thinking about starting her own business again. I guess she got burned pretty badly back in New York, but she's recovered and she likes working for herself. She and the kids bought a house about two miles from here, so we actually pass each other sometimes when we're out running."

Half an hour later, the group, which now included Nick, sat around the dining room table, eating dinner and catching up on each other's lives.

"How's the architecture business?" Nick asked as he helped himself to more bread.

"It's great," Brad replied. "That year and a half I spent selling furniture for my brother really made me appreciate what I do. The firm I'm with is small, but we're growing fast and we're bidding on a lot of new projects. In fact, the *Tribune*'s business section is doing a story on us next week."

"Emily, are you working?"

"Part time," she replied. "I took an extended leave after the second baby was born last year and ended up not going back. I still do gift baskets, but now I work at home when Zak is at school and Kayla is napping. I don't make a fortune, but we agreed that we'd live on Brad's salary and put everything I make into the bank. God forbid anything should happen, but we don't want to get caught again without enough of a cash cushion."

"How much is enough?" Nick asked.

Brad laughed. "After what we went through when I got laid off, it feels like there's no such thing as enough, but I think we're almost at the point of being comfortable enough to start making some investments. The thought makes me a little nervous, but we can't keep everything in the bank forever. We need to bite the bullet and get our money working a little harder. We've got two kids to put through college."

"Speaking of investments, I saw your brother last month, Michael," Nick said. "My girlfriend and I went to San Diego for a weekend and ran into him in a Mexican restaurant down by the bay. What are the odds of that?"

"Yeah, he said he'd seen you," Michael replied. "Did he tell you he's a big land baron now?"

"As a matter of fact, he did. He was out that night with a couple of investment partners. They were celebrating because they'd closed the deal on their fourth apartment building that afternoon. At this rate, he'll own the whole town before long."

"I think that's the plan," Michael said.

"Matt's little brother isn't doing too badly himself. These two just bought a rental house of their own," Brad said, gesturing toward Michael and Melissa.

"We got lucky," Michael said. "We had just started to look around, thinking we might dip a toe into real estate if something good came along, when we found a little place over on Elmwood that was going for a song. The elderly woman who lived there had died and her children live out of town. They just wanted to get rid of the house so they wouldn't have to worry about it, and we happened to have enough cash available to make the deal, so we're officially landlords. Or we will be when we find a tenant."

"Actually, that doesn't surprise me," Nick said, fingering his wine glass thoughtfully. "You've always been the numbers guy. You don't talk much about money, but you're smart. You've been able to avoid the trouble the rest of us have gotten into."

Michael looked at Melissa and they both burst into laughter.

"Guys, let me tell you a story."

The Secret Explained: A Few Points to Remember

- Like every other part of your life, your financial decisions should always be guided by common sense.
- If an investment or business deal doesn't feel right, it probably isn't.
- Before making an important financial decision, ask plenty of questions and get a second opinion from someone who will provide a fresh perspective.
- Remember that success is a few simple disciplines repeated over time, and failure is a few simple disciplines neglected over time.

What's Your Skinny Cow?

- Are you waiting around for a lucky break, life-altering business deal, or lottery win that isn't likely to happen rather than taking control of your financial future now?
- Are you inconsistent about applying the simple disciplines that would lead to success?
- Do you know what your values are? Do you honor them in all your business and financial decisions?

Epilogue

There is one final secret we would like to pass along.

In addition to being the best at what they do, true money masters realize that they have a responsibility to other people. Rather than keeping their knowledge to themselves and using it simply for their own gain, masters share what they know with others.

That is the final thing we hope you will take away from this book. As you apply the principles we have outlined and grow closer to becoming a money master, pass your knowledge on.

Teach your children. It's never too early for kids to begin learning about money and the good it can do.

Help your friends and family members, especially those who are struggling financially or seem to be in the dark about the need to provide for a better future. Let them benefit from what you know.

Finally, share what you have with those who are less fortunate. As your assets increase, be certain to also increase the amount you give to the many worthwhile organizations that depend on us.

Only by sharing both your knowledge and your wealth can you truly reach the level of a money master.

We began this journey by suggesting that you forget the notion of a down or up economy and instead focus on your personal, value-based economy. At the end of the day, wherever you go, there you are. So study and learn all you can, become more valuable to your family and to the marketplace and become the best YOU you can be. Let this guide you. Live Passionately—Give Radically—Love Abundantly!

Seven Questions We Should Ask Our Money Managers

Below is a list of seven questions that you should ask your money manager before you use his or her services.

1. How do you get paid? How much of your income comes from investing and how much comes from advising others?
2. Are you invested in this yourself?
3. Where will my money end up? Show me the money.
4. Is this investment suitable for my age, assets, and risk tolerance?
5. Show me your mother's portfolio.
6. Let's make a list of all the pros and cons of this investment.
7. How diversified am I? What percent of my wealth is tied up in this investment?

The Seven Biggest Money Mistakes

Below is a list of the seven biggest money mistakes:

1. **Not planning and budgeting our weekly, monthly, annual and lifetime financial goals:** 97% of households have no written plan, no budget for what they spend most of their waking hours pursuing, **money**. Not having a plan isn't a plan. Blindly acting on auto pilot like most people do with their finances is a huge mistake. Take one hour every month and 15 minutes each week to write down and review your business and personal money goals, budgets and cash flow. Designate a specific time to do this each week. Example: 15 minutes, Friday afternoon, get your entire family involved.

2. **Putting too much money on credit cards:** Most people have numerous credit cards they use without ever thinking about it. Then, the next month when they receive their statements, they are in shock as to how much they robotically charged without thinking about it. Set a budget and limit for your credit cards and track it every time

you use it. Write down the amount and the running total so that you feel it and are aware of the debt each time you use any card. There are only two things that you need to know about money mastery, the first is discipline and the second is regret. You'll either be disciplined or will feel regret.

3. **Not understanding the economic or trends that affect your money life:** Most people either look for the easiest way to invest or the latest, greatest, hottest deal. They do not understand or take time to learn about economic or demographic trends that can devastate these decisions. The aging population, global competition, and government debt can be like a 50 mph headwind working against your investment vehicles. Take time to learn, understand and think about larger economic trends that can affect your investment decisions. Things change all of the time and you must stay ahead of the curve and the herd.

4. **Buy and holding stocks:** Real wealth, real returns and real value are created through the velocity of money and investments. Buying and holding value stocks can work and could be a part of your investing portfolio. However, those stocks can represent value and equity that is not working for you at its highest and fastest rate. More than likely the institution that "holds" your stock is making money off of it every day. You need to learn and utilize the principles of the velocity of money. Equities and cash generate very little for you when they are locked away for the long term. Get your money and equity to move and generate more returns for you and your family.

5. **Failing to educate yourself on money early in life:** Where do we learn most of what we learn about finances and

money? Who taught us and why have we been taught to buy things all of the time, drown in debt, and lock our money away in financial institutions? Our financial institutions and government have taught us to do certain things with money and for whose advantage? We have to constantly question and educate ourselves as to what works best for ourselves and our family. Find out what the wealthiest people do and how they do it. More than likely it's the exact opposite of what we've all been "taught" to do. Money mastery is a lifetime practice.

6. **Trusting our financial advisors without question**: If you were told that you needed a major medical operation, more than likely you would get a second opinion. However, when many of our financial advisors recommend something, we just do it. Never be afraid to ask the tough questions of your doctors or financial advisors. We should almost always get a second opinion. Perhaps, taking an extra 30 minutes could save you from an unneeded medical procedure or losing half of your life savings. Always try to verify everything and get all promises and projections in writing.

7. **Giving total control of your finances to someone else:** Whether it's a family member, friend or financial advisor you must always take and be in control of your money. You must take the time to understand where it is, how it works and what is being done with it. Hold everyone and yourself accountable by reviewing financial documents at least monthly. Perform quarterly checkups and overviews of your progress, goals and cash flow. It's your life, it's your money, and you must be in control.

Resources and Recommended Reading

Below are some books and web sites that we suggest you read.

Books

- Alcorn, Randy. *The Treasure Principle: Unlocking the Secret of Joyful Giving.* Portland, OR: Multnomah Books, 2005.
- Blanchard, Kenneth H., and Spencer Johnson. *The One Minute Manager.* New York: William Morrow, 1982.
- Buckingham, Marcus, and Curt Coffman. *First, Break All the Rules: What the World's Greatest Managers Do Differently.* New York: Simon & Schuster, 1999.
- Collins, James C., and Jerry I. Porras. *Built to Last: Successful Habits of Visionary Companies.* New York: HarperCollins Publishers, 1997.
- Collins, Jim. *Good to Great: Why Some Companies Make the Leap . . . and Others Don't.* New York: Harper Business, 2001.
- Covey, Stephen R. *The 7 Habits of Highly Effective People.* New York: Free Press, 2004.
- Dayton, Howard L., Jr. *Your Money Counts.* Carol Stream, IL: Tyndale House Publishers, 1997.
- Fisher, Roger, William L. Ury, and Bruce Patton. *Getting to Yes: Negotiating Agreement Without Giving In.* New York: Penguin, 1991.
- Gerber, Michael E. *The E-Myth Revisited: Why Most Small Businesses Don't Work and What to Do About It.* New York: HarperCollins, 1995.
- Gladwell, Malcolm. *The Tipping Point: How Little Things Can Make a Big Difference.* Santa Ana, CA: Back Bay Books, 2002.

- Johnson, Spencer, and Kenneth Blanchard. *Who Moved My Cheese? An Amazing Way to Deal with Change in Your Work and in Your Life.* New York: G. P. Putnam's Sons, 1998.
- Kiyosaki, Robert. *Rich Dad, Poor Dad.* New York: Warner Books, 2000.
- Kriegel, Robert J., and Louis Patler. *If it Ain't Broke . . . Break It!: And Other Unconventional Wisdom for a Changing Business World.* New York: Business Plus, 1992.
- Levitt, Steven D., and Stephen J. Dubner. *Freakonomics: A Rogue Economist Explores the Hidden Side of Everything (P.S.).* New York: Harper Perennial, 2009.
- Maxwell, John C. *Winning with People: Discover the People Principles that Work for You Every Time.* New York: Thomas Nelson, 2007.
- Maxwell, John C. *The 21 Irrefutable Laws of Leadership: Follow Them and People Will Follow You.* New York: Thomas Nelson, 2007.
- McGee, Robert S. *The Search for Significance Devotional Journal: A 60-Day Journey to Discovering Your True Worth.* New York: Thomas Nelson, 2003.
- McManus, Erwin Raphael. *The Barbarian Way.* New York: Thomas Nelson, 2005.
- Rand, Ayn. *Atlas Shrugged.* New York: Signet, 1996.
- Rand, Ayn. *The Fountainhead.* Indianapolis, IN: Bobbs Merrill; Early Edition edition, 1943.
- Robbins, Anthony. *Unlimited Power: The New Science of Personal Achievement.* New York: Free Press, 1997.

Web Sites

- http://www.bankrate.com. A source for finding bank accounts, including money market accounts, offering the highest interest rates, among many other things.

- U.S. National Debt Clock—http://www.brillig.com/debt_clock. Watch how quickly the U.S. national debt is piling up.
- http://www.usinflationcalculator.com/inflation/current-inflation-rates/. General information on inflation, charts showing monthly and annual inflation rates, and a tool for calculating the inflation rate between any two years.

About the Authors

Peter Hirsch

After graduating at the top of his class from Yeshiva University School of Law in New York City, where he was an editor of *The Law Review*, Peter went to work with one of the nation's premier law firms, Cravath, Swaine and Moore. In 1992, Peter left the firm to work full-time in sales and motivational training and corporate consulting. Peter has consulted for many Fortune 500 companies and sales organizations, developing commission structures, policies and procedures, communication systems, and sales strategies. Peter is a sought-after inspirational speaker, delivering talks and trainings, ranging from keynote speeches to full weekend trainings to sales and motivational talks before audiences of up to 80,000 people. Over 1,000,000 lives have been impacted by Peter's messages on "Success by Design, Not Delusion," "From Success to Significance," "Servant Leadership," "Loyalty and Team-Building," "Living the Significant Life," "From Motivation to Mobilization," "Communication for Transformation," "The Power of Persuasion," "Live Debt Free; Live Stress Free," "Whose Retirement Is it Anyway," "The Seven Secrets of the Money-Masters," "How to Beat the Banks at their Own Game," and "Thinking Outside the Bucks—Money, Property & Eternity." His first book, *Living with Passion*, is an all-time best-seller in the direct sales industry.

Peter received his doctorate in ministry in 2001 and has developed leadership and mentoring programs for business leaders and pastors in over 15 nations throughout Africa, Asia and South America.

Peter's wealth management firm, The Leading Edge Network, is one of the most respected in the Dallas/Fort Worth metroplex, where he lives with his wife Diana and their two children, Malia and Ariel.

Robert Shemin

Internationally-respected Wealth Creation Expert and current *New York Times* best-selling author Robert Shemin first became a millionaire at the age of just 32. But he didn't want to keep all of his wealth-building strategies and financial know-how to himself. He's taught tens of thousands of Americans the secrets to attracting, growing, and securing lasting wealth through his best-selling books and countless sold-out seminars held to standing-room-only crowds in cities across the United States.

He is the author of ten best-selling books, including *Secrets of A Millionaire Real Estate Investor, Successful Real Estate Investing—How to Avoid the 75 Most Costly Mistakes Every Investor Makes, Secrets of Buying and Selling Real Estate—Without Using Your Own Money, Secrets of a Millionaire Landlord, Unlimited Riches, 40 Days to Success in Real Estate Investing,* and his newest release, *How Come that Idiot's Rich and I'm Not?*, a current *Wall Street Journal* and *New York Times* bestseller.

An expert on wealth for CNN, Robert Shemin is a frequent guest on national, regional, and local television and radio programs such as National Public Radio (NPR) and CNBC's "The Big Idea" with Donny Deutsch. He has also been featured in over 300 newspapers and magazines including *BusinessWeek,* the *Los Angeles Times,* the *Miami Herald,* the *New York Post, USA Today,* the *Wall Street Journal,* and *TIME* magazine among many others.t

With a heart as big as his bank account, Shemin gives generously to numerous charitable endeavors such as the homeless, those in need of critical eye operations overseas, and at-risk teens and college-age youth in Israel through the formation of a specialized school he founded and successfully operates. As experienced as Shemin is at showing high-net-worth individuals how to get richer, his real love is helping self-described "financial disasters" earn millions.

Robert Shemin holds a law degree and an MBA from Emory University.

Index

and personal accountability, 165
recommendations from, 19,
26–31

Gender differences in investing,
104–106
Germany, 123
Gift tax, 142
Global economy, 122–125
Goals
investment goals, 31, 33, 35, 42,
112, 113
spending goals, 49, 50
Gold
retirement plan investments
in, 23
supply of, 120
Gold standard, 120
Government bonds, 101, 125,
129, 130
Grantor Retained Annuity Trust,
141, 142
Gross domestic product (GDP)
China, 124
United States, 124

Health insurance, 86
Home office, 142

Income, tracking, 48, 49, 76
Index funds, 102, 115, 116
Indexed Life Insurance
(IUL), 141
Inflation
calculator, web site, 169
and currency, 120
and expenses, 45, 54, 55
and 401(k) plans, 137, 138, 147
and money supply, 120
and national debt, 135
and rate of return, 99
rates of, 54, 55

and retirement savings, 147
U.S. Treasury inflation-
protected securities, 101
and velocity of money, 121, 122,
134, 164
Inheritances
example, 24–42
stock, 5
and trusts, 141, 142
Instincts, trusting, 21, 39, 43, 44,
116, 117, 152, 158
Insurance
agents, 141
automobile, 46
COBRA, 86
expenses, tracking, 47
financial advisors, 40, 41
health insurance, 86
homeowner's, 142
Indexed Life Insurance
(IUL), 141
life insurance, 141
and need for cash reserves, 80
Interest, compound
and 401(k) fees, 56
and credit cards, 51, 52
and interest rates, 61
savings accounts, 51
Interest rates
bankrate.com, 83, 168
banks, 83, 84, 129–130, 168
credit cards, 51
money market accounts versus
savings accounts, 114
International investments,
122–126
International transactions, U.S.
dollar in, 120
Internet. *See also* Web sites
background checks, 17
expenses, tracking, 47
home office expenses, 143

Retirement plans (*Continued*)
Enron scandal, 21, 22
401(k) plans. *See* 401(k)
retirement plans
IRAs, 23
mutual fund investments, 17
and Social Security, 136, 137
and volatility of investments,
17, 18
Return on investment (ROI), 98.
See also Rate of return
Risk
aversion, 101
currency risk, 126
market risk, 126
political risk, 126
and reward, 99, 100, 117
tolerance, 31, 100, 101, 116, 117
Russia, 123

Safety
asset protection. *See* Asset
protection
cash, need for, 80
diversification, 21, 22, 43.
See also Diversification
importance of, 24, 43
instincts, trusting, 21, 39, 43, 44.
See also Instincts, trusting
investigation of businesses, 16
investigation of financial
advisors, 18–21, 43
investigation of individuals, 16,
17, 43
investment risk, 15, 16
overview, 43, 44
retirement plans, 23, 24
and volatility, 17, 18
Sales people
financial advisors as, 21
stockbrokers as, 21, 32, 33

Savings accounts, 101, 113, 114,
122, 129, 134
Second opinions, 151, 158, 165
Selection process for financial
advisors, 35–43
Self-discipline, 50. *See also*
Discipline
Sense
and discipline, 154, 155
financial decisions, 158
and gullibility, 150, 151
instincts, trusting, 152, 158.
See also Instincts, trusting
overview, 149–151
and trust, 151, 152
and values, 152–154
Shem, 2
Skinny cow
credit card use, 76
failure to keep money
moving, 134
failure to take control, 158
fear of asking questions, 117
fear of risk, 134
identifying, 44
inconsistency, 158
investment jargon, 117
long-term investments, 95
risk tolerance, 117
spending, 76
story of, 1–6
tax planning, 148
time management, 76
unemployment or long-term
disability, 95
values, 158
Small businesses, tax benefits of,
142–144, 148
Social Security, 136, 137
Software, 53
South Korea, 123